T0166934

PENGUIN BUSINESS

THE ULTIMATE SALES ACCELERATOR

Amit Agarwal is a *Teacher* at heart, a *Student* at mind and a *Warrior* in action.

Utilizing this *Student–Teacher–Warrior* mindset, Amit aims to harness and evangelize four life skills: *sales, mindfulness, nutritional diet* and *personal finance*. He believes that incremental progress in harnessing these life skills helps us balance material accomplishments and spiritual growth.

Amit's two books, *The Ultimate Sales Accelerator* and *Small Is Big*, are steps in this journey of evangelizing the four life skills and balancing spirit and matter.

An IIT–IIM alumnus, Amit has coined the term Salespreneur® and created a new sales strategy: Use Case Selling®. He has professional selling experience in twenty-three countries across bootstrapped and Series A, B, C and D start-ups.

Amit grew up in Jhansi, a historic town in northern India. He currently lives in the suburbs of Bengaluru amidst beautiful farmlands with his wife, Ayesha, and sons, Tanish and Aarav.

🔗 https://www.linkedin.com/in/amit-agarwal-0103643/
✉ amit.agarwal@salespreneur.in
🐦 amit_itbhu98
▶ http://bit.ly/salespreneur_youtube

ALSO BY THE SAME AUTHOR

Small Is Big

PRAISE FOR THE BOOK

'Sages and seers, through their ancient texts, conveyed how to live and conduct ourselves through cases and stories. They continue to remain etched in the mind for several years. This is exactly what Amit is conveying through "Use Case Selling". This NICE and powerful engagement tool is timely and wisely presented. It's an excellent "case" for success for every salesperson'—G. Sridhar, dean, executive education, marketing management, Indian Institute of Management Kozhikode

'What makes this book unique and memorable is that it tells true sales stories in both business and life. And through these powerful stories, one extraordinary sales strategy emerges. A must-read for all . . .' —Sam Cawthorn, CEO, Speakers Institute, and bestselling author of *Bounce Forward* and *Storyshowing*

'Amit Agarwal's book, *The Ultimate Sales Accelerator*, is fascinating and lucid. It has demystified selling. It is easy and fun to read, and if the skills described in the book are practised, the results could be extraordinary. It is based on stories of success achieved by deploying the techniques described in the book in multiple situations and contexts. The techniques elucidated in the book are field-tested, which provides confidence and nudges the reader to try them out, and thereafter improvise on the technique'— D.V.R. Seshadri, professor of marketing (practice), and director, Indian School of Business, Centre for Business Markets, Hyderabad

'This book, written by Amit, is a jargon-free, easy read, which is rare for a book on sales. It is replete with real-life, relatable experiences and examples that will be valuable for people interested in pursuing careers in customer-facing roles. Questioning for better insights and metaphors for effective communication are clearly my favourite takeaways from the book'—Rajesh Pandit, managing partner, La Hoya Business Accelerators, and visiting faculty, IIM Ahmedabad

'Practical tips from a geek's transition from deploying analytics to running multimillion sales quotas. Amit bares it all, from growth challenges, building and managing teams to scaling SaaS and consumer businesses. A must-read for modern businesses trying to build sustainable growth'— Bhavish Sood, general partner, Exponential Innovation Fund, and board member, Medimetry

'An inspiring book that illustrates how great storytelling and use cases are essential tools for an effective sales pitch. Treating a prospect as a user and not as a buyer can make all the difference. Read this book and it will help you reimagine selling. Entertaining and yet insightful!'—Hari T.N., head, HR, Bigbasket.com, and co-author of *Cut the Crap and Jargon: Lessons from the Start-up Trenches*

'Establishing trust, understanding and sharing the feeling of another, communicating one's point of view—ethos, pathos, logos—is the three-legged stool on which any agreement, any accord, sits. Amit, through examples drawn from various areas of life, personal and professional, expertly and passionately explains the science of the art of persuasion, of the business of selling'—Atul Jalan, CEO and MD, Algonomy, and author of *Where Will Man Take Us?*

'Amit has combined his remarkable in-field sales experience with a strong framework orientation and has made a compelling case for Use Case Selling. The beauty of the book lies in its startling simplicity, rich anecdotes and sharp insights. A must-read for all professionals'—Santanu Paul, founder and CEO, TalentSprint, and independent director and chairman, Innovation Council, National Payments Corporation of India

'Sales are made when a vendor's offering matches a buyer's need. While this holds true, it doesn't provide context or depth on how sellers can craft their messaging and tailor the buying experience in a modern, efficient and frictionless way. This is where Amit's work in Use Case Selling is valuable to both sales leaders and practitioners. This is a must-read treatise on modern sales, which simplifies what many in sales struggle with today: what to say and how to position the offering. Beyond this, the book provides fresh thinking and stories from Amit's extensive international career. If you seek to up-level your career in a world of information noise, Use Case Selling can help in a significant way'—Amar Sheth, COO, Sales for Life, and social selling evangelist

THE
ULTIMATE
SALES
ACCELERATOR

ONE SURPRISINGLY POWERFUL
STRATEGY TO CREATE EPIC SALES
IN BUSINESS AND IN LIFE

AMIT AGARWAL

BUSINESS

An imprint of Penguin Random House

PENGUIN BUSINESS

USA | Canada | UK | Ireland | Australia
New Zealand | India | South Africa | China

Penguin Business is part of the Penguin Random House group of companies
whose addresses can be found at global.penguinrandomhouse.com

Published by Penguin Random House India Pvt. Ltd
4th Floor, Capital Tower 1, MG Road,
Gurugram 122 002, Haryana, India

First published in Penguin Business by Penguin Random House India 2022

ISBN 9780143460435

Typeset in Aldine401 BT by MAP Systems, Bengaluru, India

www.penguin.co.in

This book is dedicated to my parents

My mother's name is Asha,
which means Hope;
my father's name is Vinod; it means Joy

May this book usher Hope and Joy into your lives

My Wish for You

Thank you for choosing this book 🙏

May this book help you:

✓ Create EPIC sales in business and in life.
✓ Understand the deeper meaning of sales and harness it as a life skill.
✓ Become a Salespreneur®.

Contents

To My Reader

'Life is about creating and living experiences that are worth sharing'

—Steve Jobs

What makes each one of us unique?
As I reflected on this question, I asked more questions.

Is it our physical appearance, our speech or the roles that we perform?
I heard my inner voice saying 'No', as people may have some similarities in how they look, how they speak and what they do.

Is it our financial status?
No.

Is it our life experiences that are very personal to us?
Yes. Yes. Yes . . .

The answer was a resounding 'Yes', and I felt happy and contented with it.

Each one of us has our own life experiences, wherein we have seen failure and success.

A combination of these life experiences makes us knowledgeable, wise and unique.

> *'Experience is the teacher of all things'*
> —Julius Caesar

I believe that a book offers a beautiful opportunity to share our own unique experiences with others.

As you read this book, you will notice that each chapter contains real-life experiences from my professional and personal life. It also narrates the experiences of many other people when it helps to endorse a point that I am making.

Three chapters (chapters 4, 5 and 6) have been specially curated with experiences in business-to-business (B2B), business-to-consumer (B2C) and personal life situations. These real experiences validate the universal nature of the sales strategy unveiled in this book. There are specific exercises, which are called **Learning Accelerators**, given after each chapter for you to validate and experience your learnings. The **checklist** introduced in chapters 4, 5 and 6 can be used to analyse any sales scenario in our business or personal life.

Thanks a lot for choosing this book and let's start our exciting journey of exploring the 'One Surprisingly Powerful Strategy to Create Epic Sales in Business and in Life'.

Preface to the Expanded and Updated Edition

The first edition of *The Ultimate Sales Accelerator* was published in July 2019.

Since the release of the book, I experienced a set of life-changing events:

1. **Book Reception**

   I was filled with gratitude for the reception received from the book's readers. The book became #1 on Amazon Hot New Releases in the pre-order period itself.

The book got 100+ Amazon reviews within a few months of its launch. Here are a few of the reviews.

'. . . In a true sense, this book is "The Ultimate Life Accelerator"'
—Ashish Mishra

'The best sales book I have ever read'
—Neha Agarwal

'This book is superb in that it brings structure and predictability to a function as disorganized as sales'
—Vishal

In addition to Amazon and Goodreads, readers used LinkedIn to share their learnings and experience.

Rohit . • 1st   • • •
Co-founder at famepilot.com | Automated Reviews Management SaaS | Cust...
3yr • Edited • 🌐

Reading Amit Agarwal's The Ultimate Sales Accelerator is like driving the Ferrari of Sales. I guess It's one the best Sales learning book in Indian perspective. Concepts like Use case selling, The One thing, Storytelling are very well explained. It does not give any theoretical gyan, It provides practical how to-do methods to apply, which are required for an Entrepreneur or a Sales Person.

https://lnkd.in/fu5ntqR

Highly Recommended !

Anil Saighal   2y   • • •
NLP Trainer & Success Coach for Business, Leadership and Holistic Development.

The Ultimate Sales Accelerator by Amit Agarwal is not just a book.

It is an education in Sales & Communication.

It is a course, it is a workbook and it is a complete process by itself.

As a first-time author, it was a surreal experience 😇.

I am grateful to the readers and the community for giving me such a memorable experience 🙏.

2. Pandemic

The COVID-19 pandemic changed the world and expedited the adoption of virtual selling.

3. Training

I took 100+ training sessions in offline and online set-ups using the teachings of *The Ultimate Sales Accelerator*. Interactions with participants were an enriching experience.

The updated and expanded edition captures my deep reflections and implementation learnings while experiencing the above-mentioned three points. In the expanded and updated edition, we:

✓ Introduced a *new chapter*: 'How Does Use Case Selling Accelerate Virtual Selling?'
✓ Added readers' success stories, FAQs, a sales prayer, one suggestion to get the most out of this book and an index to the key concepts, frameworks and accelerators used in the book. This is part of the *bonus material* section.
✓ Added *videos* to explain key concepts. You can access them by scanning the QR code. Using offline and online content available in the book, you can have an immersive and deep learning experience.

✓ Updated the *Insights* section in Chapter 2. It now covers three types of insights.
✓ Corrected minor spelling and grammatical mistakes in the first edition.
✓ Updated a few other sections.

I hope that the expanded and updated edition of *The Ultimate Sales Accelerator* helps you create EPIC sales in business and in life. Happy reading!

Prologue

Four Scenarios and Four Questions

'People don't buy what you do; they buy why you do it'
—Simon Sinek

Sometimes we experience scenarios that look different and yet they lead us in the same direction to find something significant. I experienced four such scenarios . . .

Scenario 1: India's Software Product Story

India is recognized as a great success story in the world of IT and business process management (BPM) services; these sectors have clocked a revenue of $167 billion by FY18–19.[1]

The changing landscape has given rise to many product start-ups in these segments in recent times. In India, 7200–7700 tech start-ups were incepted during 2013–18.[2]

As I reflected on the rise of product start-ups, a question came to my mind.

How can software product start-ups in India be recognized as world-class companies and create a sustainable growth ecosystem?

As I reflected on this question, the answer emerged in the form of the following 2x2 matrix:

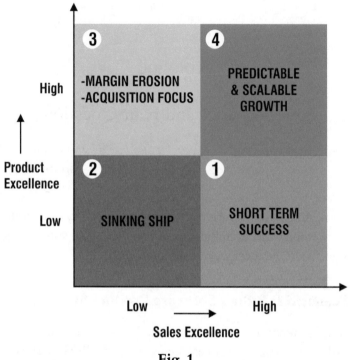

Fig. 1

The next question that came to my mind was . . .

What sales strategy will help an organization move to quadrant 4?

Scenario 2: Communicating with Growing Kids

My elder son became a teenager in January 2019. My younger son is around nine years old but he speaks like a teenager. I have seen how difficult it is becoming for my wife to communicate with them.

'Please don't play video games for more than thirty minutes.' 'Please don't use bad words.'

'Don't fight with each other.'

These are just a few of many situations that my wife and other mothers face daily and I saw it as a challenge.

When I reflected on it, a question came to my mind.

How can my wife and other parents communicate effectively with their kids?

Scenario 3: Angry and Disappointed Colleague

While sitting across from Amar, my office colleague, in a café, I could see anger in his eyes.

'My salary has increased by just low single digits for the last two years. I am putting in so much hard work. My boss doesn't understand at all.'

As I empathized with Amar and reflected on his predicament, I wondered,

How can Amar develop persuasive communication skills to communicate his ideas effectively?

Scenario 4: Changing B2B Sales Ecosystem

The pandemic (COVID-19) changed the way we sell. Gartner says that 80 per cent of B2B sales interactions between suppliers and buyers will occur in digital channels.[3]

As I reflected on this new data point, I asked . . . *Who is the sales owner of the future?*

Each of these four scenarios asked a question.

Can this book give you One answer for all four questions?

Chapter 1

Why This Book?

'Judge a man by his questions rather than his answers'
—Voltaire

I am a big fan of asking questions because I believe questions create infinite possibilities. If I were to make a statement, you would have two choices. You can either agree with what I say or disagree with what I say. Instead, if I asked you a question, you could arrive at an answer based on your personal notions and experiences. This is why I keep asking questions in different scenarios. Every chapter of this book is asking and addressing a question. And, interestingly enough, it was a set of questions that gave birth to this book.

In 2016, I saw a video called 'The 3 Most Important Questions to Ask Yourself'.[1] In the video, Vishen Lakhiani (CEO and founder of Mindvalley[2]) asks his listeners to answer three questions and he gave them ninety seconds for each answer. He asked us to write down the answers without thinking too much. The questions were as follows:

What would I like to **experience** *if time and money were not in question?*

What are the various ways I would want to **grow**?

What are the ways I would want to **contribute** *to this world?*

I did this exercise and kept the answer sheet in a drawer in my study. For the third question about the ways in which I would want to contribute to the world, I answered, 'Publishing a book' among my other dreams. When I wrote these words, the seed of becoming a published author was sown in my mind. And for this realization, I am deeply grateful to Vishen Lakhiani.

While the seed was sown in 2016 through this wonderful exercise, the growth of the seed is attributed to another experience. The credit for the growth goes to a life-changing book. *Have you ever come across a book that has made such a profound impact on your life that you turn to it whenever you seek guidance?* For me, that book is *The One Thing*[3] by Gary Keller and Jay Papasan. This book helped me to direct my energies in the right direction by positing this one, beautiful and powerful question:

What is the one thing I can do such that by doing it, everything else is easier or necessary?

Such an impactful question, isn't it? After reading this book, I developed the habit of asking this **one thing** question in many aspects of my life.

Reflecting upon these two significant experiences, I am reminded of this quote by Neale Donald Walsch:

'I tell you this: There is no coincidence, and nothing happens by accident. Each event and adventure is called to your Self by your Self in order that you might create and experience who you really are.'

Vishen Lakhiani's video and the book, *The One Thing*, came into my life for a reason. While the former's wonderful questions sowed the seed, the book provided the required manure for its growth. What was left was watering the seed and that happened over a meal.

One morning, over breakfast with my wife, a thought occurred to me. What if someone asked me, *'If you were to share only one simple thing that has contributed the most to your success in sales, what would that be?'*

Interestingly, the answer came to me faster than I had expected and it was Use Case Selling®! This unexpected answer brought a smile to my lips and I decided to write a book because a book offers an amazing opportunity to connect with an infinite classroom.

How I Discovered Use Case Selling

Daniel Pink, the author of *To Sell Is Human*, says, 'We're all in sales now', and I wholeheartedly agree with this statement. I have been successfully selling for many years now. On the business front, I have sold in twenty-three countries across North America, Asia, the Middle East, Africa and Europe over the last twenty-plus years. In my personal life, I continue to sell as a son, husband, father, friend and employee. So, as you can see, my experience in sales goes back nearly two decades but the significant turning point came just a few years ago. **It was only in 2015 that I discovered that one approach to sales, which would open huge windows of possibilities for me, both professionally and personally. And that approach is Use Case Selling!**

In May 2015, I joined a start-up that was planning a major pivot. Till then, this company was offering managed services to enhance user experience and personalization to the e-commerce and travel industry. They were aiming at a massive change that would involve the following new items:

- A new industry vertical called financial services (banks, insurance, securities, mutual funds)
- A new, subscription-based revenue model that takes the subscription fees in advance as opposed to the managed services model
- A new product offering in the form of a marketing automation platform

At this point in our journey, we had no customer references and our product was at an early stage of its development. Considering our position as a start-up and the competition we were facing from large software vendors such as Adobe, Oracle, Salesforce and IBM, this was a David and Goliath situation. To handle such a situation, I was looking for a sales strategy that would be simple, powerful and effective. And incidentally, I found this fresh line of action during a client meeting.

I had a meeting with the chief marketing officer (CMO) of a very large bank in Asia. I arrived fifteen minutes early and was asked to wait in the conference room. As I waited there, many questions went through my mind. I thought, 'I represent a start-up but here I am meeting executives from one of the largest banks in Asia. This is a great opportunity. How can I create value for the attendees? How can this meeting be impactful?' Needless to say, I was both excited and nervous! In exactly fifteen minutes, about six or seven sharply dressed executives entered the room. After the usual exchange of pleasantries and business cards, the discussion started.

The CMO started with a short sentence that would have put me on the back foot if it hadn't been for the power of Use Case Selling.

He said, 'Our company works with the best software in the world for analytics and customer experience. We have IBM, Adobe and SAS.'

There are times when you can feel unspoken words and on this particular occasion, I could hear the CMO saying, 'Why are you here?'

His demeanour did not fluster me and I said, 'May I ask you three questions?'

The CMO said, 'Sure!'

'Could you please tell me the number of unique visitors visiting your bank's website every month?'

'12 million,' the CMO answered.

'*And among these 12 million visitors, are you able to separately identify the existing customers and the ones new to the bank on your homepage?*'

The CMO was unprepared for this question. He looked around the room to consult with his subordinates. 'No,' he answered quite dejectedly.

'*And are you able to **personalize** the website experience for your existing customers?*'

At this point, the CMO's face and tone betrayed his anger and annoyance. 'When I cannot identify the existing customers on the website, how can I possibly customize their experience?' he said.

Yes, I had addressed the elephant in the room. I could immediately sense certain dissatisfaction in the room with respect to the capabilities of their current software. There was an uncomfortable silence in the room and the rest is history. The CMO's company emerged as one of our most important clients and we often used this story as a reference for several potential clients.

Of course, as an employee of the start-up, I was elated with the results of the meeting. The sales professional in me was intrigued by the dynamics of our conversation. I've had several successful meetings in the past but something felt different. I gave this interaction with the CMO and his team a thorough thought. I asked myself, 'Why did this meeting go so well? What did I do differently?'

My questions yielded the following answers:

I had put forward a question that helped in revealing the **unknown** need of the client.

I shared something **insightful** that the CMO wasn't aware of. The language of the conversation was **lucid, easy to follow** and **free of technical jargon**.

My second and third questions gave rise to anxiety and aspiration in the client. He was **emotionally** charged and that made him quite angry.

I smiled to myself and with a hint of pride said, 'This meeting is a wonderful Use Case of how clients can be engaged effectively.'

And as soon as I uttered the words 'Use Case', I felt a certain warmth and positivity. It rang a bell and excited me. It was an aha moment for me and the term 'Use Case Selling' was born. Since then, it has become an integral aspect of my life. I have used Use Case Selling in multiple scenarios in both my professional and personal life, and it has resulted in the following developments:

- ✓ I have developed a great rapport with my family and have been able to inculcate some great habits like financial discipline and good hygiene in my kids. And how did I manage to do so? You will find out in the subsequent chapters.
- ✓ My income has tripled in three years.
- ✓ My organization has achieved 100 per cent YoY growth. Its deal sizes were up to five times that of other start-ups.
- ✓ My team was able to successfully negotiate with clients within a difficult industry vertical (financial services) globally without even having a physical office in many countries.

✓ My team was able to close large deals (> = \$5,00,000) during the pandemic without meeting the client.

And all this happened because of Use Case Selling! Magical, isn't it? Sometimes I wonder what would have happened if I had stumbled across Use Case Selling before 2015. I cannot imagine the kind of value addition it would have made. Now, let's not dwell on the past. We can only live our present to the fullest. And therein lies the importance of my book. I want to assist every individual who is determined to sell his or her idea, product or service with integrity and cohesiveness.

If you think about it, you will see that each of this world's 7.7 billion people is in sales.

- A child is asking his father to buy an expensive video game.
- A mother is telling her son why too much chocolate is bad for his teeth.
- A sales director is giving a software demo to his prospective clients.
- An employee is giving her manager reasons why her salary should be increased.
- A politician like Barack Obama is giving an inspirational speech.
- A CEO is launching a product.

What is the one common theme that you come across in all of the examples mentioned above?
They all involve **connecting with people** and influencing them to take a decision. In our various roles,

we are selling either a product or a service or an idea. **Thus, we all are in sales, and sales is a life skill.**

This book has many examples of Use Case Selling being successfully implemented in spheres like business-to-business (B2B), business-to-consumer (B2C) and even in our personal life. Through this book, I wish to help everyone understand and use this powerful tool to enable **epic sales** in business and in life. And what do I mean by the term epic sales? It means making a sale against all odds such that it becomes a great milestone.

Do you recollect the legendary story of David and Goliath? An epic sale is like that story where David emerges victorious . . . a victory that was both improbable and created a milestone.

Decoding the word 'EPIC'

Scan the QR code to watch the video

Learning Accelerator

1. What are the three sales scenarios in your life—be it products, services or ideas—that you are finding difficult to achieve?
Sales Scenario 1

_____

_____

_____

Sales Scenario 2

_____

_____

_____

Sales Scenario 3

_____

_____

_____

2. What does epic sales represent? Please tick mark the boxes.
   ☐ Milestone
   ☐ Something very easy
   ☐ Memorable
   ☐ Something very difficult
   ☐ David and Goliath story

Chapter 2

What is Use Case Selling?

'To build trust with customers, one thing sales owners can do is to move from "Always be closing" to "Always be connecting"'
—Amit Agarwal

The phrase 'use case' has its origins in software engineering and system engineering. In 1992, a book called *Object-Oriented Software Engineering: A Use Case Driven Approach* popularized the technique for capturing the functional requirements in software development. However, other than in engineering, I have come across 'use case' in the following contexts:

*Can you show me a live **use case**?*
In this case, use case refers to a credible example.

*I have a few **use cases** to discuss. Can you come and meet me?*
In this case, use case refers to requirements.

*Let's not talk in vague terms. What's the exact **use case**?*
In this case, use case refers to bringing in clarity through clear examples.

11

To summarize, a use case generally stands for a good example that addresses a specific requirement and brings clarity. Traditionally, it was used more for requirement analysis rather than selling. In the context of this book, **we will make use of the term 'Use Case Selling' to denote a holistic, four-pillared approach to the world of sales.**

Use Case Selling discovers a specific unmet need of the user through a simple conversation or by telling a short story, which offers the user an insight and invokes an emotional state of aspiration or anxiety.

So effectively, Use Case Selling sees the Customer as a User (participant) rather than a Buyer.

From the above definition, we can come up with a useful little acronym that perfectly tells us the four pillars of Use Case Selling. That acronym is **NICE**. It can be expanded as:

Fig. 2.1

NICE is the best way for us to remember the four pillars of the Use Case Selling strategy.

The four pillars are listed in the above diagram. Let's study each in finer detail.

NEED

We all have needs. And our needs can be categorized into **Serviced Needs** and **Unserviced Needs**. This categorization is very important for Use Case Selling. If you refer to the diagram below, you can think of the concept of needs as similar to climbing Mount Everest. Just like climbing Everest, addressing the four human needs becomes more difficult yet more rewarding with every step. Now we'll look at a few examples of each kind so that we can identify the type of need with ease.

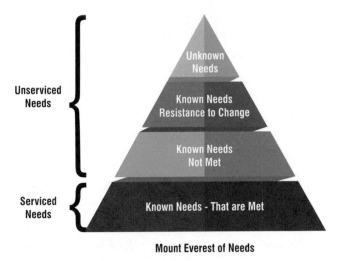

Mount Everest of Needs

Fig. 2.2

Serviced Needs: Known Needs That Are Met and Are Serviced Well

This kind of need is simple. It comprises needs that have come up in the past and have been met effectively. Let's look at a few examples . . .

Power steering in most cars to make driving easy and comfortable.

Remotes for switching on televisions and changing channels. I remember how painful it was to do that with a black-and-white TV.

A cable TV HD recorder to pause and record live content allows viewers like me to watch something whenever I am free and to fast forward the advertisements.

Unserviced Needs

Unserviced needs are needs that are not yet serviced and await fulfilment. We may be aware of these needs (known needs) or we may not even be aware of these needs (unknown needs).

Unserviced needs can be subdivided into three categories:

Known Needs That Are Not Met as Yet, or Are Not Serviced Well

Example 1: Verizon's 2001 TV commercial, 'Can you hear me now? Good!'

Roughly two decades before cell phones were in the early stages of their use, a known need of many consumers was to have a reliable mobile phone for personal and professional purposes. Users were tired of calls dropping, lack of clarity during conversations and erratic connections that couldn't be relied upon.

It was Verizon Wireless that addressed this 'known but unmet need' in 2001 through a series of TV advertisements titled, *'Can you hear me now? Good.'* In the campaign, the protagonist went to unlikely places like potholes, mountains and snow peaks and said, 'Can you hear me now? Good.'

Using a single statement, Verizon captured the requirement and the interests of the users in a crisp yet compelling manner. The success of the advertisements was rooted in the sheer simplicity of their tagline, the visual element and the direct fashion in which they addressed the problem of poor connections.

1   2

Example 2: Making the daily commute to work easier and more productive.

Remember the long hours commuting when you had to drive in bumper-to-bumper traffic to get to work every morning? For a long time, easy commuting was an unmet demand and office-goers continued to suffer as the traffic grew day by day, making it a nightmarish experience to get to work. Finally, Uber addressed this unmet demand and introduced its operations in India. Ola too joined in. I don't remember driving to work for the past three years. Taking an Uber or an Ola is always more relaxing and convenient. By ensuring that the commute is hassle-free and comfortable, Uber and Ola have increased the productivity of office-goers. Gone are the days of being tired before even reaching your workplace!

Known Needs Where the User Resists Change or Refuses to Adapt to a Situation

We have needs that we are aware of but we do not pursue them either due to a lack of complete information or because we resist change that requires us to step out of our comfort zone. Here are a few examples:

1. Waking up at 5 a.m.

Don't we all wish to be up by five every morning? But how many of us can confidently say that we have done so, consistently? Waking up early is a nightmare for most of us. We do not want to step out of the comfort of a warm blanket and embrace a healthy lifestyle. I, too, have tried my hand at this and I failed. It was finally on 2 January 2018 that I successfully joined the 5 a.m. bandwagon. And how did I successfully do so? I asked myself the simple question:

What is the one habit I can develop in 2018 such that by developing it everything else would be easier or unnecessary?

The answer was simple. Wake up at 5 a.m.!

2. Video Engagement

During the pandemic (COVID-19), sales owners couldn't meet customers in person. A lot of sales owners got depressed because of this change. In such a scenario, video engagement platforms (Loom, Vidyard, etc.) enabled sales owners to record videos and share them with their customers. Videos humanize selling in a remote context. While this was a clear need, several sales owners initially resisted this change due to past habits.

Unknown Needs That the User Is Completely Unaware Of

If we take the time to compare our current lifestyle to our life five years ago, we would be surprised at how much everything has changed. A piece of technology that we may use every day may not have been around back then. What has happened here? Some product or service came about and made us aware of a dormant need that we were not aware of and successfully serviced it. These are unknown needs that the user is completely unaware of.

Blackberry

Blackberry emerged as a status symbol for business executives from 2005 to 2012. The phone had all the features of a great communication device as well as the added advantage of providing easy access to emails. This combination is an example of servicing an unknown need of a business executive who cannot lug around a desktop or a laptop but needs to be in constant touch with his or her work.

Apple TV and Chromecast

Almost a decade ago, could you think of going through your photographs and streaming content directly from your cell phone on a digital media player? It was definitely an unknown need for users like me, who were unaware that content could be streamed in such a way! So you can imagine our surprise and excitement when Amit Gandhi, a dear friend from the US, gifted us an Apple TV! Back then, it hadn't been launched in India and we were thrilled to see how we could watch YouTube videos and our photographs on this amazing device. Something that wasn't even a known demand seven to eight years ago has now become a part of our daily lives. Funny, isn't it?

What is the Mount Everest of Needs?

Scan the QR code to watch the video

INSIGHTS

'If you always do what you always did, you will always get what you always got'
—Albert Einstein

This quote by Albert Einstein effectively explains the rationale behind any human liking new things. It also highlights the importance of this often-used phrase, 'Tell me something I don't know.' **Insights help users/buyers to appreciate new ideas and embrace unknown possibilities. And it is only when they open their minds to new ideas that they will receive fresh experiences and advantages.** Another real-life experience will help me elucidate this better.

During a trip to the beautiful hill station of Munnar in Kerala, my wife and I visited a tea factory where they explained the entire process of manufacturing tea. They told us about the various stages and how different parts of a tea leaf were used to make different varieties of tea. For the first time, we stumbled across something called *white tea*. My wife and I looked at each other, surprised and curious to know more. We were then told that white tea is the variety that has been through the least degree of processing. It is light to taste and has several health benefits. We were quite happy and ended up buying a packet of white tea. It is to be noted that initially, we had no plans to buy tea and all we had in mind was a visit to the factory. So how did we end up making that purchase? This is because our guide shared an interesting insight regarding the product, which we were previously unaware of. This insight moved me to take action and buy the product.

The following picture summarizes the benefits of insights to buyers and sellers.

BUYER BENEFITS	SELLER BENEFITS
1. Rapport Building	1. Trusted Adviser
2. Memorable Experiences	2. Increased Conversion Rate
3. Creation of a Buying Vision	3. Decreased Sales Cycle

Let's understand the three types of insights.

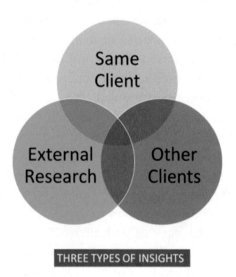

Fig. 2.3

Insight Type 1: Same Client

*When a client says, 'I learnt something valuable about **my** own business that I didn't know.'*

To make this possible, the sales team must develop a deep understanding of the client's business. This is possible via preparation, extensive research and engagement during the sales cycle. Deep engagement during the sales cycle can be achieved through workshops, product trials, demos, questionnaires, checklists, etc.

One exciting way to understand your client's business is to experience it from a buyer's perspective. If possible, experience buying your client's product or service. Let me share an example.

My demand generation team failed to get the meeting with a marquee insurance company after trying many times. To get a meeting with this life insurance prospect, I created a PowerPoint presentation (deck) in December 2016, featuring my experience of buying term insurance on its website. I shared the deck via email with the chief digital officer (CDO), head of analytics and head of digital marketing. Each slide of the deck had a headline and a screenshot of what I had experienced on the insurer's website. I have copied the exact headlines from the slides in the deck; only the name of the insurance client has been changed.

Slide 1: I went to Pinnacle Life website
for an online term plan on 5th December

Slide 2: I chose 1.5 cr Cover for 30 years
and got an annual premium of
Rs 21,247. I didn't proceed further.

Slide 3: I then went to Pinnacle Life
website many times and didn't
see any 1:1 personalized banners
using my premium amount of
Rs 21,247. Saw a general banner as
given below

Slide 4: I got a call, received an email and also
received an SMS

Slide 5: Since I was travelling internationally,
I couldn't respond

Slide 6: I have been browsing the Internet
since Dec 5 and have yet to see a
display banner

Slide 7: The following 1:1 personalized
banner on paid media will excite
Pinnacle Life Prospects including me.
Isn't it?

Slide 8: The following 1:1 personalized
banner on owned media will excite
Pinnacle Life Prospects including me.
Isn't it?

Slide 9: <Client A> reduced their COA
by 75% using 1:1 personalization

What COA reduction does Pinnacle Life want?

INSIGHT

Are you curious to know what happened after I sent the email?

The email was sent at 7.07 p.m., and the client CDO responded at 7.26 p.m., the same day.

We got the meeting and signed the deal in the next three months.

The buying experience deck was insightful for the CDO because I shared my experience as a buyer and identified gaps and solutions as a growth marketing evangelist. It created both aspiration and anxiety for the CDO and his team. This prompted client action that led to closure of the deal.

As is clear in the above example, an insight unearths acute problems that the customer didn't know before or didn't consider earlier.

During client interactions, I have used a checklist as one way to discover hidden problem areas with a client. It has three columns: requirement, current adoption and relevance. As clients fill out this checklist, both the client and the solution provider will discover many of the things that they don't know.

S. No.	Requirements/ Use Cases	Current Adoption	Relevance
		High/ Medium/Low	High/ Medium/Low

The word 'curated' is crucial here because a checklist should contain use cases/requirements that matter most. This comes from deep analysis and preparation at the solution provider's end.

Insight Type 2: Other Clients

*When a client says, 'I learnt something valuable about **other** businesses that I didn't know, which is relevant to my business.'*

Sharing relevant insights and implementation experiences from other clients can trigger client response and lead to deal closure. Here is an example.

In 2016, I met a prospect, Satya, VP, digital marketing of a large bank in Asia. Satya liked our discussion, and he immediately took me to meet his boss, Varun, chief customer experience officer. I shared how other banks (same segment) were personalizing offers for every customer on the home page of their website. Varun liked the idea a lot and said, 'Wow, I didn't know that this is possible and other banks are adopting this use case.' He asked me to keep sharing such use cases from the banking industry. At his request, I shared an email with the subject line *God Level Personalization* after a few weeks. This email covered the experience of a banking customer after experiencing personalization on his bank's website.

I got a call from Satya.

'What have you done, Amit?'

Surprised, I asked, 'What . . .?'

'Why did you share the email?' asked Satya.

I said, 'Because Varun asked me to do so . . .'

'Yes, but now he is after me that other banks have moved ahead, and we are still behind . . .'

In this true example, sharing insights from other clients created growth and novelty in the first meeting with Varun and FOMO (fear of missing out) because of the email I had shared. Did we sign the deal? Yes, we did.☺

To enable this type of insight, the solution provider needs to analyse three items within existing clients: *Adoption, Impact and Innovation (AI^2)*.

✓ Adoption: Which capabilities/use cases are adopted, and which are not?
✓ Impact: What is the impact created quarter on quarter?
✓ Innovation: Which capabilities/use cases create novelty and a wow factor?

Quarterly business reviews (QBR) with existing clients help the solution providers measure and share AI^2. AI^2 results in insights, which can then be shared with prospects.

Insight Type 3: Research

*When a client says, 'I learnt something valuable via **research** that I didn't know, which is relevant to my business.'*
Research can be from industry bodies such as Gartner, Forrester, McKinsey, academic institutions, etc. Research can also be carried out by the solution provider.
Let me share an example.
With one of our retail clients, we have repeatedly evangelized the narrative of the connected experiences by Forrester.
We showed the Forrester diagram that explained connected experiences. Connected experiences are about delivering integrated experiences on both inbound (website, app) and outbound (email, SMS,

app notification, etc.) communication channels. This retail client had all the individual software modules for inbound and outbound personalization but they were not connected. Rather than pitching a replacement of individual modules, we pitched our integrated solution using Forrester's connected experiences narrative. It was a pleasant surprise that the client started using the connected experiences terminology and created a business case for this internally. The client also did three workshops with us to finalize connected experience use cases relevant to them.

Having understood the three types of insights, please ponder on the following question:

Which of the three insights is most difficult to curate?
1. Same Client   ☐
2. Other Clients ☐
3. Research   ☐

Tip: The Venn diagram used for insights in Fig. 2.3 is to remind readers that they can *combine* and deliver different types of insights.

A simple checklist for the efficacy of insight:

S. No.	Insight Benefit	Insight Attribute	Adoption
1	Learning	Customer learnt something new about their own business and found it valuable OR Customer learnt something from other business and industry sources and found it valuable	
2	Novelty	Customer experienced the following: 'Wow, I didn't think about it' rather than 'That's correct, I have thought about it in the past'	
3	Action	Customer reciprocated and acted positively after the insight was delivered	
4.	Memorable	Customer remembers the insight later	

Some of you may be wondering, 'How do we make the insight-sharing process easier?'

The following three ways will help:

✓ Cultivate insight sharing as a habit

Before going for any discussion, ask: *'If I have to share only **one** valuable insight with the audience, what would I share?'*

✓ Insight repository

An insight repository helps the sales team

1. Find insights across diverse scenarios in one place
2. Share individual learnings across the team
3. Train and onboard new team members

Here is a simple template of insight repository:

S. No.	Shared By	Insight Description	Insight Type	Client Name	Impact

✓ Insight-sharing sessions

To inspire each other and enable knowledge-sharing, insight-sharing sessions among the sales team need to be scheduled once per month or once in forty-five days or at least once a quarter.

When sales owners deliver authentically provocative insights, the buyer experiences respect for the sales owner, aspiration/anxiety for the solution and a strong desire to act.

Conversations and Short Stories

Conversations

Have you ever wondered why we always think of a question as the easiest way to start a conversation? When we are meeting new people, we always ask them, 'Where are you from?' Isn't that a great conversation starter?

Interestingly, to understand the power of a question, I had to ask one! Consider it as a question about questions.

Why do questions work in the context of sales?

When I tried to think of the answer, the two words that came to my mind were **Possibilities** and **Participation.** The beauty of a question lies in its capacity to create possibilities and elicit participation.

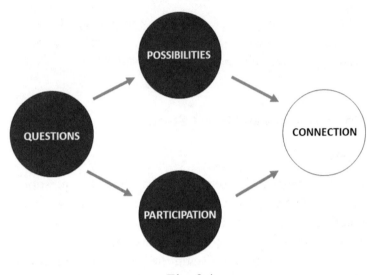

Fig. 2.4

Imagine you are meeting a group of kids and you tell them, 'The sky is blue.'

Now that's a statement. There is nothing more to it.

But what if you ask them, 'What colour is the sky?' One kid may say it is blue. A few others may say it is black at night. Some may say that the sky has different colours throughout the day. Just look at the vast possibilities a simple question can create.

Imagine that you are addressing a seminar on sales for 300 attendees. You have two options at hand to start your speech:

Option 1: 'Sales is a life skill.'

Option 2: 'Is sales a life skill or a profession?'

It is no surprise that the second option is your obvious choice. By starting with a question, you will generate participant engagement as your audience will now interact with you and not just attend the seminar as passive listeners.

Short Story

> *'People do not buy goods and services. They buy relations, stories and magic'*
> —Seth Godin

Why are humans fascinated by stories?

As I thought of a possible answer to this question, I was immediately reminded of my grandmothers and my mother, who told my siblings and me wonderful stories when we were growing up. Until the time my two sons became teenagers, I used to tell them two stories every day. These experiences made me realize that stories are an integral part of almost every individual's childhood. Our first tryst with stories happens through our families. As we grow up, the human relationship with stories blossoms with films, books, television shows and our interactions with so many fellow travellers in this journey of life.

So what is a good story?

A good story, like a bedtime story, is simple and experiential. And the stories and conversations used for Use Case Selling should strive to be like that.

So, what do we mean by simple and experiential?

Simple: A simple story is **relevant** to the user. The language is easily understandable and doesn't make use of technical jargon.

While telling a story, we are inclined towards telling our version of the truth. However, if we want to be relevant to the user, we have to understand his or her experiences, needs and notions and illustrate their version of the truth. And one of the most effective tools to simplify complex ideas is to make use of metaphors. A metaphor is a figure of speech that equates two dissimilar things for the sake of comparison or symbolism.

> 'The greatest thing by far is to be a master of metaphor; it is the one thing that cannot be learnt from others; and it is also a sign of genius since a good metaphor implies an intuitive perception of the similarity in the dissimilar.'
> —Aristotle

We often say, 'Don't fight like cats and dogs!' That's a metaphor.

To highlight the enormity of a $1 trillion debt in simple words, US President Reagan said in 1981, 'A trillion dollars would be a stack of thousand-dollar bills sixty-seven miles high.'

Now if you are wondering if you can use metaphors in business communication, the answer is a big YES! A creative metaphor can be a very effective tool for influence and persuasion in business. A few real situations will help you understand how we can use them.

At one of the organizations I worked with in the past, we were working on the customer experience on the website of a leading bank in India. The analytics department of the bank was reaching out to my team for various requirements on data enrichment. While this was not our main offering, we were helping our client to the best of our capacity. Although we had communicated to the bank that their requirements couldn't be met, our team continued to receive repeated requests from the client. During a quarterly review, I met their head of analytics.

I asked him, 'Do you enjoy films or cricket?'

'Both,' he answered with a smile.

'Great,' I continued. 'Since you like films, you definitely agree that Amitabh Bachchan is the superstar of Indian cinema. And I am sure that a leading bank like yours would want to work with software providers whose profile is similar to that of Amitabh Bachchan in their field. **So Abhay, we are the Amitabh Bachchan of website personalization. When it comes to data enrichment, we are like the new actors in Bollywood.'**

It is interesting that after this meeting, the client understood that our distinct forte lay in website personalization and they didn't pursue the question of data enrichment as they had done before. This single metaphor helped me in my interaction as here Amitabh Bachchan was symbolic of excellence in the field.

During a negotiation meeting in the Middle East, I told my client, 'Our software is like Mercedes-Benz at the price of a Toyota Corolla.' This statement immediately lightened the atmosphere and put my clients at ease. This helped me greatly.

Clients have also shared their woes using interesting metaphors. I once met a prospect whose organization had been working with another software partner for the past three years. When I asked him about his experience with them, he said, 'Amit, it is like driving a Ferrari in the narrow lanes of Mumbai.' I could immediately sense his pain.

Experiential: The story engages visual and auditory senses, and evokes feelings. It creates a contrast to involve the user. You will notice that most successful films employ concepts like 'hero versus villains, 'poor versus rich', 'sadness versus happiness' or 'good versus bad' to establish an element of difference. It makes the plot more compelling. **Relevance** and **Contrast** are the two key factors that make a story truly captivating for its audience.

Keeping in line with the themes of relevance and contrast, we can incorporate the concept of 'Don't Tell, Show Me Your Story' to enhance the experience of the user. And one of the most effective examples of this is a video called 'How to Move People with Your Story'. In the video[3], Lisa uses her own inspirational tale of fighting against all odds to demonstrate the difference between telling your story and showing the same. You will be able to make out the difference once you've read both:

How Lisa Tells the Story

'There was a time in my life that was very difficult, very challenging and very uncomfortable. I didn't have a lot of money. I didn't have a lot of hope and things just looked dismal. At some point, I had to turn my life around. At some point, I made the decision that life had to get better.'

How Lisa Shows the Same Story

'Six days a week I had to eat beanies and weenies. I had to find money in the crevices and the corners of my couch so that I could get milk for my son. There were times when my heart would beat fast, just at the thought of what I was going to eat tomorrow. At some point, I got sick and tired of my own story. Is this going to be my future? No, I can't handle it.'

Clearly, **showing** your story is much more impactful than simply narrating it. Don't you feel more connected to the second script? The video is even more powerful because of the use of hand gestures, facial expressions and tonality.

Emotion

'Real persuasion comes from putting more of you into everything you say. Words have an effect. Words loaded with emotion have a powerful effect'
—Jim Rohn

Tony Robbins, a leading authority on peak performance, rightly says, 'Motion creates emotion.' Our changing physiology has quite a significant effect on our emotions. Think about it. After a vigorous workout session at the gym, don't you feel positive and energized?

Interestingly, I have found the opposite to be true as well. ***Emotion too creates motion.*** A simple story will help you understand how an authentic emotion can create a powerful and pleasantly surprising motion. In this case, the resultant motion is an action or a sale.

On 28 July 2018, my younger son, Aarav, turned nine and we gifted him a Nintendo Switch for his birthday. Strangely, this present was not even in question about a month ago when he first mentioned it to me. So how did we get here? Before letting you in on my son's trade secret, let me share a few words of Aristotelian wisdom. Aristotle spoke of three modes of persuasion. They are as follows:

Ethos: Highlighting the credibility of a presenter

Logos: Use of logic, data, facts, figures and statistics

Pathos: Appeals to the emotions of the audience (sympathy, anger, feeling vulnerable, aspiration, anxiety, etc.)

So a month before Aarav's birthday, Aarav spoke to his mother about his gift. He wanted a Nintendo Switch. My wife directed the conversation to me. I had just returned from a long tour and was tired when he brought it up for the first time.

'Daddy, you gifted Tanish (elder brother) a Sony PS4 on his tenth birthday,' Aarav said.

'Yes, beta (son); the tenth birthday is a milestone.'

'I understand. May I have a Nintendo Switch for my birthday?'

At that point, my two primary concerns were regarding the pricing of the Nintendo and the fact that we already had a video game in the house.

'But Aarav, we already have a PS4. Why don't you buy something else?'

'I know we do, but I want a Nintendo because the games are different from those on PS4. It doesn't have fighting games like PS4. Mario is awesome!' (Logos)

I will be honest that the reasoning of a nine-year-old impressed me. I reluctantly inquired about the price of the gaming console.

'Around Rs 30,000 for the gaming console and Rs 10,000 for two games. I need two games,' Aarav said.

Needless to say, I was extremely shocked at how expensive it was. To be honest, I almost fainted! Somehow, I regained my composure and said, 'Beta, this is extremely expensive for a ninth birthday present. We can talk about this next year when you turn ten. But now is not the time.'

'Daddy, why don't you gift me this now and next year, I will choose something regular.'

By that time, Aarav had turned down all my reasoning. I had to be more firm with him and reiterated in a slightly raised voice, 'No, beta. This Nintendo Switch is way too expensive. I think you should look for something else that you might want and we will get that for you.'

Aarav looked disappointed, but he let it go. I too felt bad but I thought that it would eventually be all right. But the next day, my wife told me that Aarav was very upset. He has always been a peaceful boy but on this occasion, he had cried. He felt that I was ready to gift his elder brother what he wanted but I wasn't prepared to do the same for him (Pathos). The fact that my son had shed tears over this matter upset me even further.

In this emotional state, I decided to do my research and compare the prices available on Amazon and then in Dubai and the US. There was a certain degree of positivity that was coming about when I began looking around for a reasonable deal. Aarav too aided the process by giving his inputs and watching out for offers. Soon enough, he found a great deal on Amazon India where we were saving about Rs 10,000. I immediately purchased the Nintendo Switch. And you can see my son's happiness in the picture.

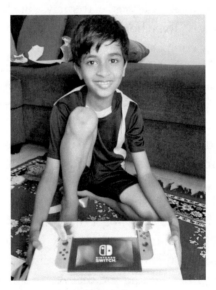

Fig. 2.5

After I purchased the game, the sales professional in me wondered how this nearly impossible sale took place successfully. Initially, I was quite sold on the idea of not buying something so expensive. In the end, we went ahead with it and it turned out to be quite a reasonable deal. **The answer to this question is pathos or the mode of persuasion that appeals to the emotions of the buyer.** Pathos evokes anger, sympathy, inspiration, vulnerability or even anxiety. Naturally, a nine-year-old made use of an appropriate pathos to make an impossible sale in less than thirty days. As you can clearly understand from this real-life example, emotions can work wonders for anyone trying to make a tough sell.

Our emotional state can thus be categorized into two:

The emotion of growth or gain: Aspiration
The emotion of loss or pain: Anxiety

Which one among the two is stronger? Let's have a look.

In 1979, psychologists Daniel Kahneman and Amos Tversky published the Prospect Theory. It is also known as the Loss Aversion Theory. The theory stated that humans are two to three times more likely to take a decision or seek a risk to avoid a loss than to achieve a gain. As evident in the graph, the loss-value curve is steeper than the gain-value curve. Simply explained, a person who lost $100 would lose more satisfaction than a person who had a windfall gain of the same amount. This clearly tells us that the anxiety corresponding to a loss is a stronger emotion than the aspiration connected to a gain. Insurance companies capitalize on this emotional curve by asking you if you have protected your family. The fear of your loved ones suffering drives you to purchase an insurance policy. They arouse anxiety in the mind of a concerned family man and drive him to action.

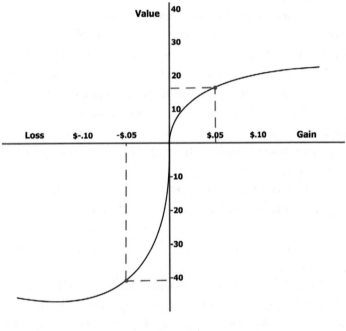

Fig. 2.6[4]

The power of Use Case Selling lies in the combination of these four pillars, i.e., NICE. It efficiently combines a short story or conversation, a specific and unserviced need, an emotional state and an insight into one package and creates an engaging experience for the user. This user experience drives epic sales.

USE CASE SELLING SUMMARY VIEW

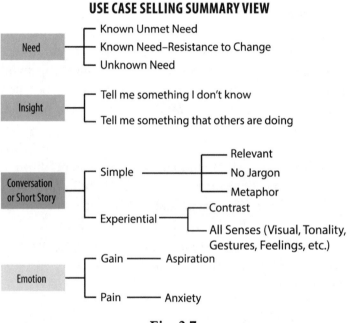

Fig. 2.7

In the previous chapter, I had spoken about my meeting with the CMO of a leading bank. A quick recap of the conversation will help you follow better. I had asked the CMO three questions. They were about the number of unique visitors on their website, if they were able to identify the existing users from the new ones and subsequently, customize the website experience for the former. We found out that until then, the CMO's company hadn't been able to identify them or customize their experience.

Now, let's identify the four pillars of Use Case Selling in my interaction with the CMO.

Need: Out of the three questions, the CMO could answer only one to his satisfaction. The need of the company to identify existing customers from the website and then personalize the experience for them was yet to be fulfilled. It was an unknown need.

Insight: The CMO acquired fresh knowledge through my questions. Questions 2 and 3 helped him understand that they could not personalize the experience of their existing customers on their website because they couldn't identify existing customers among website visitors. Among the three types of insights, this is type 1: Same Client.

Conversation or Short Story: My interaction with the CMO lasted for about five minutes. I asked only three questions. The language was easy to follow, simple and free from technical jargon. He listened with rapt attention during the entire five minutes.

Emotion (Aspiration/Anxiety): The bank in question was one of the largest banks in Asia. Needless to say, they were working with the best software. Yet, the CMO was quite angry and dejected when he had to answer the second and third questions with a no. He realized that despite spending so much time and money buying 'world-class software', they were yet to identify their existing customers and customize the banking experience for them.

To my readers who are gradually getting a grip on the concept, I would like to reiterate that Use Case Selling is a very simple method. It is powerful yet easy to use. It is layered yet smooth to grasp.

Through the chapters that follow, you will see:

- How I have used this strategy in my professional and personal life
- How a few companies across the world have an inherent Use Case Selling approach.
- How book readers have implemented Use Case Selling

I will take you through many more interactive and relevant examples and by the end of it, you will be a master of identifying and using Use Case Selling!

Learning Accelerator

1. What are the four pillars of Use Case Selling?
    N = _____
    I = _____
    C = _____
    E = _____

2. Go back to the three unachieved sales scenarios we
    identified in chapter 1.
    Now reflect . . . have you built all four NICE pillars
    into your sales strategy?
    Which one is missing?

3. Think of one situation in your personal
    and professional life where you bought
    something—a product, service, or idea.
    Can you identify the NICE pillars in that experience?

4. What are the key components of a powerful story?
    ☐ Jargon
    ☐ Contrast
    ☐ Metaphor
    ☐ Simple language
    ☐ Many messages

☐   Makes the reader experience with more than one
     of his or her senses (visual, auditory, feelings, etc.)
☐   Relevance to the listener
☐   One key message

5.   Emotion creates _____.

6.   Which two aspects does the insight pillar cover?
☐   Tell me something I don't know
☐   Tell me how you will solve my current
     requirements
☐   Tell me something that others are doing
☐   Tell me more about your product features

7.   Can you find the word 'CONVERSIONS' in the
     following word?
     CONVERSATIONS

Chapter 3

How Use Case Selling Is Different from Other Forms of Selling

'Features don't sell. Benefits sell sometimes. Use cases always sell'
—Amit Agarwal

As you would have noticed by now, I'm fascinated with Use Case Selling! Yes, it is a concept very dear to me and has helped me immensely. But as I said, it was only in 2015 that I came across Use Case Selling as a definitive strategy in sales. Till then, my team and I had used many methods to make sales. This chapter seeks to bring about a thorough comparison among the different forms of selling and in the end, lets you decide whether Use Case Selling is indeed different and more impactful than the others.

The two forms of selling that are going to be discussed apart from Use Case Selling are **Features Selling** and **Benefits Selling**.

Features Selling focuses primarily on the specific capabilities of a product. And to explain its features to the user, the selling technique often involves the use of technical jargon that the user may not understand. Consider these examples:

This cloth is made up of polyviscose fibre

Toyota Altis Engine has 103 kW (140 PS) at 6400 rpm

As a user, do terms like polyviscose fibre and 103 kW (140 PS) at 6400 rpm encourage you to engage with the product? Or do you feel slightly lost and unable to understand the product?

Benefits Selling focuses primarily on results.

Imagine a financial planner telling you, 'If you invest with us, we can ensure promising returns of up to 18 per cent!'

The planner's claim will immediately give rise to questions in the mind of a rational consumer. *Does this sound too fast? Does it seem too direct? Do you feel engaged?*

Now, someone may be interested in taking it forward and would like to talk to the planner to gain more information. But many of us will shrug off the offer and think of it as a pure sales pitch. Thus, benefits selling may or may not be an engaging experience for the user. It can end up being too direct, only focusing on the gain without addressing the pain (need) of the consumer and is often at the expense of user experience.

In contrast to the aforementioned strategies, **Use Case Selling focuses on establishing a deep and trustworthy connection** with the users using the four NICE pillars of need, insight, conversation/story and emotion. *The strategy approaches a customer as a user and not as a buyer.*

At this point, a question may arise in your mind: **What is the difference between a user and a buyer?** Don't we use these words interchangeably? Interestingly, there is quite a lot of difference between the two. Two real-life stories will help you understand when you are a user and when you are a buyer.

In 2018, my family moved into a four-bedroom, three-storied villa from a smaller two-bedroom apartment. After a couple of weeks, a sales representative from Eureka Forbes visited our home. Eureka Forbes is a company dealing with water purifiers, air purifiers, vacuum cleaners and security solutions. My wife asked me to meet them and see their live demo. At that point, I thought that it wasn't required because we had already employed enough domestic help to clean the house. I asked my wife to politely send them back. However, she was curious about seeing the demo.

'Amit, why don't you just meet them? They are already waiting.'

Reluctantly, I agreed. I went downstairs to see a team of two sales representatives waiting. Quite surprisingly, they did not start off with the usual discussion on cleaning the floors. Instead, they asked me a question.

'*Do you clean your sofas and curtains regularly?*'

In my head, the answer was a clear no! But my wife said, 'We have just moved into this house. All the curtains and sofas are brand new.'

And then before our eyes, they vacuumed our sofas and curtains and showed us the amount of dust that had accumulated in apparently brand-new curtains and sofas. My wife and I were shocked to see this. The man also explained to us the other uses, such as cleaning fans, cars and finally, floors. But they had successfully convinced me the moment I saw the amount of dust in our sofas and curtains.

So what had worked in their favour?

The sales representatives from Eureka Forbes had created an insightful experience for us and addressed a need that I was not aware of. The dust created anxiety in our minds, as this was extremely detrimental to the health of the family. Moreover, the live demo added the much-needed visual element. They showed it to us instead of just saying something. So yes, we bought the vacuum cleaner although I was previously against the purchase. In this case, the sales owners approached a user at a time when he had no intention of buying their product. **We were just users, yet to be transformed into buyers.**

As evident in the Eureka Forbes vacuum example, **being early in the sales cycle helps in finding the prospects as users and not as buyers.** In B2B sales parlance, we often ask, *'Are you writing a request for proposal (RFP) or responding to an RFP?'* When we engage a prospect as a user early in the sales cycle, we write the RFP. But there are times when we cannot get there early enough and we meet a buyer, not a user. **A buyer has a fair idea of what he requires.** Now, can we transform a buyer into a user in such a situation? Yes, we can! In this case, we need to challenge the status quo in a positive way and offer fresh insights that the user may have missed out on or was completely unaware of.

Let me explain with an example from my personal life. My family wanted to gift me a bicycle on my birthday.

We all went to a popular sports store in Bangalore called Decathlon. My son had been using a gear cycle for the past four years and it served his purpose. We started looking around for geared cycles and the prices ranged from Rs 10,000 to Rs 64,000! Honestly, I was overwhelmed by the fact that a bicycle could end up costing as much as a motorcycle. I could sense that my family was very keen to gift me this. I asked the store salesman for help.

'Sir, do you want to use a bicycle for adventure, exercise or recreation?' he asked.

'Mostly for recreational purposes but also to get some exercise.'

'And how many kilometres do you plan to use it for?'

Since I was planning to start bicycling after twenty years, my target wasn't too ambitious.

'Around 1 to 3 km.'

He then showed us a couple of regular bikes that didn't have gears.

'But these bikes are without gears,' my son said.

'Yes, they don't have gears. Since Sir is planning to use it for recreational purposes and for a maximum distance of 3 km, a bike without gears will work perfectly well. You can ride up to 7 km a day with ease. A gear bicycle is good for adventure sports. Moreover, the geared ones need more maintenance.'

So what happened here? I had entered Decathlon as a buyer who was looking for a geared bicycle. The salesman at the store asked me the correct questions and ascertained my actual need, which was a bicycle for recreation that could work very well up to 3 km. Keeping in mind these requirements, he made me realize that there was no need to invest in a geared bicycle. He then shared an insightful rationale regarding when to buy a non-geared bicycle and when to go for a geared bicycle. His insights transformed me from a buyer to a user. And as a user, I purchased a non-geared one at Rs 8000, which is a reasonable amount and would beautifully serve my purpose.

The following table highlights how the approach of a sales owner should differ while addressing a user and a buyer:

When the Prospect is a User	When the Prospect is a Buyer
Focus on addressing needs that the users may not be aware of	The buyer will have his or her initial requirements ready and thus the focus will shift to addressing the known needs of the user
Create a competitive advantage	Create a 'me too' effect
More possibilities for making a connection	Pressure of closing

Let's take a final example to understand what a customer will experience when all three strategies are used to make a pitch.

The Buying Experience of Visitors Who Revisit an Insurance Website

Imagine three sales professionals making a one-minute pitch to the head of e-commerce of a life insurance company. Each person employs one of the sales techniques.

Sales Owner 1 uses Features Selling: We can provide the real-time segmentation feature for your website visitors.

Sales Owner 2 uses Benefits Selling: Personalizing the experience of your website visitors in real-time will give you three times the existing level of growth.

Sales Owner 3 uses Use Case Selling: Let's study the buying experience of your online users. A user comes to your website and generates a life insurance quote of Rs 12,833 for a term of thirty years. But this user didn't buy the policy. When this user revisits the website, the website recognizes the user as a past visitor and shows the same premium of Rs 12,833, prompting him to buy it now. But unfortunately, your current website doesn't offer this user experience. I have experienced this myself.

Which of the three short pitches captivates your interest? Definitely, the third one, isn't it? My team and I have used all three forms of selling. It is a well-known fact that every time we try selling by using pitches based on the features or benefits, we feel a clear lack of interest. The client's body language suggests that we are wasting his or her time. But in the case of Use Case Selling, our client is connected and the sale has progressed.

The table below summarizes the differences between the three approaches:

Criteria	Use Case Selling	Features Selling	Benefits Selling
Identifies unfulfilled need	Y	Nil to limited	Limited
Creates engaging user experience	Y	N	Nil to limited
Develops rapport	Y	N	N
Shows results	Y	N	Y
Uses technical jargon	N	Y	Sometimes
Evokes an emotion of aspiration	Y	Nil to limited	Y
Evokes an emotion of anxiety	Y	Nil to limited	N
Shares insights	Y	N	N
Includes stories or conversation	Y	N	N
Contrasts between the current situation and the desired situation	Y	N	Nil to limited

Thus, when we compare Use Case Selling with Features Selling and Benefits Selling, the first thing one will realize is that it is a more engaging and holistic approach to sales. This approach completely engages the user and establishes a connection through the skilful use of the four NICE pillars. This is why it is applicable in various sales scenarios such as business-to-business (B2B), business-to-consumer (B2C) and also in personal life. We will now see many examples of Use Case Selling in all three categories.

Learning Accelerator

1. Please pick the right option.
   Use Case Selling sees a customer as a
   ☐   User
   ☐   Buyer

2. Is there a situation in your business or personal life, where you have been pitched a product, service or idea and you were not convinced? What did the salesperson use—Features, Benefits or Use Case Selling? Which NICE pillars were missing?

   _____

   _____

   _____

   _____

   _____

   _____

   _____

   _____

   _____

Chapter 4

How Use Case Selling Works in Business-to-Business (B2B) Scenarios

'Approach each customer with the idea of helping him or her solve a problem or achieve a goal, not of selling a product or service'
—Brian Tracy

Business-to-business (B2B) sales are considered to be quite a complex phenomenon due to the involvement of more people, procurement processes, regulatory requirements, knowledgeable buyers in an information economy and other difficult dimensions. Most importantly, B2B sales involve the dynamic element of human-to-human interaction. People buy from people. So for a successful B2B sale to happen, you need to build a rapport and connect with the people you are working with. In this scenario, Use Case Selling works wonders. It makes the B2B sales process easier and more predictable. Let's have a look at how this happens through real-world examples that I curated from my personal experiences in sales.

When a Potential Client Became the Salesperson

Have you ever been in a situation where instead of the sales professional making a pitch to the customer, the customer sold an idea to the sales owner?

This happened when the head of the e-commerce wing of an insurance company persuaded me to create a solution that I believed I wasn't ready to. To understand the context better, let me explain the meaning of the term **'Retargeting'**.

Have you ever seen a product (phones, garments, books, etc.) on an e-commerce website but not purchased it on the first go? Later, you saw the advertisement for the same product (phones, garments or books) while browsing other websites or while on Facebook. You may then have clicked on the advertisement and made the purchase. This is a way of engaging prospects and converting them into customers. In the space of technology solutions, this is called Retargeting.

For a substantial period of time, my company was servicing e-commerce clients using retargeting. Steadily, we reached a point where we wanted to explore fresh ideas. Our company was pivoting from being a point solution (retargeting) company to a holistic marketing automation suite company. We created a different division within our company to handle the marketing automation business for clients from financial services.

One of the leading insurance companies in India got in touch with our division to undertake retargeting for them. But I wanted to approach this project using the marketing automation approach and not retargeting.

I told them that we could help them only via a marketing automation suite and not retargeting. My sales owner was clearly disappointed by my initial approach. Nonetheless, he was unrelenting. The client insisted on having a thorough discussion with me after which I would be free to take the call. I agreed to this and a call was fixed.

'Amit, we want you to do retargeting for our website visitors.'

'Thanks for your interest in retargeting. But this division handles the marketing automation platform. We would be happy to serve your personalization needs across different channels using the same,' I answered.

'But we want only retargeting, Amit.'

'In that case, I can refer you to the other division that focuses only on retargeting.'

Very interestingly, the client was convinced that the division handling retargeting wouldn't be able to handle their retargeting requirements. He continued to share his company's needs. His persistence was intriguing.

'Amit, think of this scenario,' he said. 'A user comes to our website to buy car insurance. He chooses the Honda Civic and gets a premium of Rs 11,000. But he does not complete the purchase and leaves the website. Using the common methods of retargeting, we will now show the user a couple of generic advertisements. But we want to revamp this existing idea. When a user visits other websites, we want to show him an ad that has **the Honda Civic and the premium amount of Rs 11,000**. Later, we want to show the user the colour of the car. In this way, each user will have a 1:1

personalized experience. This will vastly improve the customer experience and will increase our online conversions.'

The moment I heard this wonderful idea, I was enthused to start working on it. I realized that the insurance company wanted an **e-commerce-like personalization** for their customers. To the best of my knowledge, this Use Case wasn't live in the insurance industry. I decided to get on board and create this kind of personalization for my clients.

'Yes, let's do it!' I said enthusiastically.

Later, our involvement with this project became a key differentiator for us. It also became a credible reference for our agility and innovation.

Now let's analyse this using the Use Case Selling model.

Need: The client shared his requirement, which was yet to be met. His requirement also addressed an unknown need within me to do something innovative for the insurance industry. This was a unique case where both the buyer and the sales owners had unfulfilled needs that were being met.

Insight: I hadn't thought of using car models, colours and insurance premium amounts for personalizing the user experience in the insurance industry. My interaction with the client gave me a fresh insight into this.

Conversation/Short Story: This conversation was for five to ten minutes where both my client and I were completely involved. The client shared a short story about the current user experience and how they wanted to bring about a change in it. It showed a clear contrast.

Emotion (Aspiration): I was very happy and extremely excited at the thought of being the first company to address this unserviced requirement of the insurance industry. This would help us to explore broader avenues and serve as a credible reference.

When a Client Said 'Yes' to Our Software Even Though They Had Existing Software

We were already working with leading banks in Asia and we were eager to expand our operations. So I met the head of digital of another major bank. Satya was impressed with our work. But he was unclear as to how to take our interaction forward as the former head of digital had already purchased software quite similar to ours. I think it was this interesting background that made our interaction even more memorable.

'Satya, I understand you have already procured customer experience software and you are in the process of implementation,' I confirmed.

'Yes, that is correct,' he answered.

'May I share a list of use cases that will improve your customer experience? Since you have already made an investment, you can see if these use cases can be made live using your existing software,' I said.

My words definitely surprised Satya. 'Of course, this would be very helpful!'

So I walked him through the use cases and my team even presented the same to him in a document form. Some of them are as follows:

Use Case 1: Nitin Shukla, an existing customer of the bank, has a pre-approved car loan of Rs 12,00,000. When Nitin Shukla visits the bank's home page, he is greeted with a message that welcomes him and also a banner highlighting the pre-approved car loan of Rs 12,00,000. While browsing LinkedIn, Nitin also sees a personalized advertisement that says, 'Pre-approved car loan of Rs 12,00,000.'

Use Case 2: Atul Sharma is an existing customer of the bank and is browsing the most premier credit card on the bank's website for about ten minutes. Yet, he doesn't submit a lead. Using this signal, a message is sent to Atul on his email, via SMS and an app notification. This message conveys the benefits of the credit card.

Use Case 3: A new user spends five minutes on the credit card section of the website and doesn't submit a lead. In the external digital ecosystem, this user's profile is that of a 'traveller'. So while browsing through other sites like NDTV or Forbes, the user sees an advertisement highlighting how that particular credit card will make travelling easier.

After our first meeting, I received a response from Satya about three months later.

'The use cases shared by your team are very useful. Unfortunately, they cannot be implemented by our current software. And even if it can happen, it will not be for another one or two years. How soon can you implement these use cases using your software?'

I could sense mixed feelings within Satya. He was disappointed because the existing software would take quite some time to update itself. But he was fairly positive about starting innovative work with a new team.

'Satya, as we have done similar work for other banks, a few of the use cases can go live from the first month itself!'

My words made Satya very happy and we embarked on this project.

Now let's analyse this, using the Use Case Selling model.

Need: The use cases shared with the bank were relevant. They addressed a known need, where there was resistance to implementing a change because the existing software was already in place.

Insight: The customer learnt of multiple new requirements and was surprised to know such use cases were already being used by banks.

Conversation/Short Story: In this example, two different conversations were involved. But no technical language was used. The two interactions with Satya created a contrast in the mind of the user, differentiating his present state from that of the future.

Emotion (Anxiety): The client was very anxious that either our use case ideas couldn't be implemented by their current software or it would take quite some time for it to happen. The fact that existing banks were way ahead of them in terms of personalizing their website experience also made it more urgent for them to catch up.

When a Client Remembered the Software Demo Even after One Year

We were serving a famous bank using our personalization and customer experience platform and I also happened to be a customer of the same bank. So I would often use my personal experience on the bank's website to engage potential clients. My live demo would go something like this.

Step 1: I would visit the bank's website in the presence of the client.

Step 2: I would log in.

Step 3: I would log out and then return to the homepage.

Now, the homepage would greet me with my name and the specifics of my personalized offers like a car loan of Rs 22,00,000 and a personal loan of Rs 6,00,000. This unique personalization would greatly impress clients who saw it happening before their eyes!

I conducted the same demo with a bank in the UAE and they were very happy with our work. They too signed up as our client. One year later, I met Vivek and Madhu during an event in Dubai. They worked with that bank in UAE. I had interacted with Vivek before; he had been a key decision-maker during our previous interactions. The conversation that followed is a memorable one.

As Vivek introduced me to Madhu, the latter said, 'Amit, Vivek has been a great champion of your company's work. He knew that most of us had accounts with the same bank that you used to show the demo. He asked us to log in, then log out and revisit the homepage to see the personalization happening. We hadn't seen anything like that before. Vivek popularized the use case by asking all of us to experience it ourselves. By explaining it to us in the way it was explained to him, we all became great admirers of the kind of work that your company has been doing.'

I was humbled and amazed when I heard how much Vivek had loved our presentation and work. I thanked him profusely. Every sale brings in interesting nuances and this one was certainly in line with 'When was the last time I experienced something for the first time?'

'Amit, I remember you logging in to your online banking account and jokingly telling us not to see your bank balance. It was a very simple and powerful demo highlighting a key use case. I just replicated it with my colleagues and that helped in building a business case,' said Vivek.

Now let's analyse this using the Use Case Selling model.

Need: Personalizing the experience of their customers was an Unknown Need as it was not live anywhere in a bank in the UAE.

Insight: The clients were introduced to two new concepts. One, banks using their homepage for personalizing the customer experience. Second, an existing customer of an Indian bank was live-streaming his experience on the website in front of everyone.

Conversation/Short Story: In less than two minutes, I had shown my experience of being an existing customer of the bank. It was a true story that was being shown to them and not just told to them. Vivek liked it so much that he asked his colleagues to try the same and was appreciative of the Use Case even one year later.

Emotion (Aspiration/Anxiety):

Aspiration: Banks in India have this kind of personalization. We can be the first ones in the UAE to have something similar.

Anxiety: If we don't bring in innovative changes in customer experience, our bank will be left behind in the race.

I hope that I have been able to underline the advantages of using the use case approach in B2B sales through these real-life examples. The key element in B2B sales is ensuring continuous client engagement. Use Case Selling makes this engagement easier through the four pillars. Can you imagine what would be the result if any one of the four pillars were missing in our interactions with our clients? The success of it lies in the synergy of the unserviced need, offering an insight, engaging in conversation and evoking an emotion.

Learning Accelerator: Identify the four NICE pillars of Use Case Selling in the above example.

When a Customer Asked Me to Stop Our Engagement

A reputed insurance company in Asia had been our client for almost two years. One fine day, I received a message asking me to meet them. I was worried because they didn't mention the reason for this sudden plan. At their office, I was greeted by Nitin. He was the head of e-commerce and appeared to be very serious even when pleasantries were exchanged.

'Amit, whatever we have achieved through your company can now be achieved via other leading players in the market. They are meeting us every day and can deliver within a month. We want to start working with them and stop our engagement with your company.'

Naturally, Nitin's words came as a complete shock. I was upset and shaken. For a start-up, it is of paramount importance that we retain every customer and this was one of our most strategic clients. I knew that I had to gather my wits and make a valid point.

'Nitin, can I wear the hat of a marketing solutions expert rather than the head of customer success of my company and carry on this meeting?'

'Sure,' Nitin said.

'In marketing, AI stands for artificial intelligence. For me, A stands for Automation and the I is for Integration. In the last six months, we have focused on integration. Is that correct?'

'Yes, we were focusing on the integration of data and communication channels.'

'So now it is time to focus on the automation part of it. I want to ask you a few questions in this regard.'

'Please go ahead.'

'Do you know the preferred channel of communication for each of your customers? For example, do you know if a customer loves communicating via email more than SMS, website and mobile apps?'

'No . . . Not as yet.'

'Okay. Now if you send a message based on the channel preference of the user, will it aid in customer engagement?'

'Of course, it will,' Nitin answered.

'Great; now imagine finding a preferred channel where sending messages to each customer is completely automated and your team doesn't have to worry about it.'

By now, Nitin was curious and hopeful. 'Is this possible?' he asked, the excitement evident on his face.

'Yes, very much so,' I said. 'This is what our new automated orchestration will help you achieve. If you implement it, this is going to be a first in the country. I doubt if true AI-based orchestration is possible via any other vendor. And if any other vendor can achieve the same at a lower cost and in less time, I suggest you part ways with us and go for the new company.'

'This is interesting. When can we start with automated orchestration?' Nitin asked.

As you can guess, our association with them continued and we went on to work on the project with great enthusiasm.

Learning Accelerator

This effective checklist will help you identify the Use Case Selling elements in any given sales situation. To practise, please fill out the following Use Case Selling checklist for the previous example.

The Four Pillars of Use Case Selling	Y/N	Comments
Need		
Addresses a specific, unserviced need (known need that is not met OR known need that resists change OR unknown need)		
Insights		
Shares valuable information that the customer doesn't know		
Shares valuable information about what other players in the market are doing, including client success stories, market research and analysis		
Conversation or Short Stories		
Uses questions and/or stories and/or metaphors and/or visuals to involve the user		
Does not involve any technical jargon		
Establishes a contrast to highlight the gap between the existing state and the desired state		
Emotion		
Triggers emotions of aspiration (gain) and/or anxiety (pain)		

Chapter 5

How Use Case Selling Works in Business-to-Consumer (B2C) Scenarios

'Every sale needs to address 3 Ws: Why buy?,
Why buy now?, Why buy from you?'
—Amit Agarwal

As compared to B2B, B2C sales have a much larger market. Why is that so? This is because each of the 7.7 billion people in this world can double up as your customer. Companies like Samsung, Apple, Procter and Gamble, Airtel, Verizon and Citibank are examples of companies in the B2C space. They provide some of the most essential goods and services without which it is almost impossible to function in our day-to-day lives. And can we implement Use Case Selling in B2C? I'll let you be the judge of that after we discuss a few interesting examples.

Steve Jobs' iPod Launch

In 2001, Steve Jobs launched the iPod, a brainchild that single-handedly revolutionized the world of music.[1]

During the launch, he said, *'Boom, that's the iPod. I have one right here in my pocket. Here he is, right here.'*

He then proceeded to take out the device from his pocket and held it up for the crowd to see. It was met with laughter and applause. The audience instantly connected with Jobs, his style of addressing the crowd and of course, the product itself.

'This amazing little device holds 1000 songs and it goes right into my pocket.'

Fig. 5.1

In just a few words, Jobs conveyed the significance of the iPod. It instantly engaged the people present. Imagine yourself in the audience. Wouldn't you be enthralled by this product that you can carry around with so much ease? For music lovers across the world, the iPod was massive news. This short iPod pitch is one of the best examples of Use Case Selling.

Need: Steve Jobs was addressing a known but unmet need. Everybody wanted a handy device with good storage capacity, which would enable them to enjoy all their favourite music on the go.

Insight: The fact that 1000 songs could be stored in a pocket-sized device was previously unheard of. The audience gained an insight into the new technology that would make their lives easier.

Conversation/Short Story: In a matter of ninety seconds, Steve Jobs successfully established contrast, using the aspects of volume (1000 songs) and size (it will fit in your pocket). This is something you haven't heard of before and at the same time, you want it. He then showed the iPod to everyone present in the room, establishing vivid imagery.

Emotion (Aspiration): Wow! 1000 songs in my pocket! This attractive feature of the product evoked an immediate desire and awe in the minds of the audience. Steve Jobs used the principles of 'Seeing Is Believing' and 'Show, Don't Tell' to emotionally capture the crowd.

Apple's 'Shot on iPhone' Campaign

The iPhone 6 was released in September 2014. Six months later, Apple launched a second campaign called 'Shot on iPhone 6'. They collected photographs captured by the iPhone 6 from seventy-seven photographers across seventy cities in twenty-four countries and it was a major success.[2]

So what was so special about their campaign?

They did not talk about the features of the camera like sensors and megapixels nor did the campaign contain a picture of the phone. What made it click? It was the simplicity and the brilliance of the message. **The ad had a visual image, a tagline that hits the message and the name of the photographer.** These three elements were enough to captivate the onlooker.

I remember the first time I saw the advertisement outside Mumbai Airport. I was amazed and very happy. The photograph was so vibrant and it was very surprising to know that such clarity could be achieved on a phone camera. Now we could take professional photographs during my holidays without having to carry an expensive camera, which is quite cumbersome. I would no longer require any special equipment or extensive technical knowledge to take great photographs. An iPhone 6 will do all of that for me. So using just one image, a simple one-liner and the name of the photographer, Apple achieved all four dimensions of the Use Case structure:

Need: The string of advertisements addressed a known but unmet demand. People wanted their phone cameras

Apple's 'Shot on iPhone' Campaign

Fig. 5.2

Fig. 5.3

to be as good as, if not better than, professional SLRs and DSLRs. iPhone also democratized photography as a profession because you no longer needed to buy expensive equipment.

Insight: Just like me, many users could never imagine such beautiful and large hoardings to be the product of a phone camera. It was something new and incredible. The use of big billboards was a brilliant idea to highlight Apple's superior innovation and expand its reach.

Conversation/Short Story: The 'Shot on iPhone' campaign is perhaps the shortest message I have seen for Use Case Selling. The message, the accompanying visual and large billboards were the key elements. They were relevant to the user and effectively showed the contrast between a normal phone camera and an iPhone camera.

Emotion: When a user with an iPhone sees an ad for the same, it results in a feeling of pride and aspiration. When a user who doesn't have an iPhone sees the same ad, it causes jealousy or appreciation. Both emotions can give rise to the need to purchase an iPhone.

It is no surprise that this campaign won the top prize in the Outdoor Cannes Lion Grand Prix in 2015.[3] Juan Carlos Ortiz, the president of the jury at Cannes, defined it as a game changer. 'It's really opening a new way of doing things and changing behaviour,' said Ortiz.

How an Innovative Start-up Sold Me Financial Planning Even When I Was Afraid of Financial Planners

My experience with financial planners has not always been pleasant. I had a very small portfolio of equity stocks with a financial advisory company. A financial planner from the same company coaxed me into investing Rs 2,50,000 in the commodities market. He promised an annual return of 35 per cent. Of course, it was foolish on my part to accept this claim. A year later, I tried getting in touch with him but he did not answer his phone. I was really surprised and contacted the company. I was informed that he had left the organization. Not only that, my investment now amounted to zero. I felt angry, betrayed and let down. I realized that it was the result of my own foolishness. Nonetheless, it was upsetting. So when I was approached by this financial planning start-up, I was very sceptical. I agreed to open an account in December 2016 but I asked for a call only after five months. That is when I had a word with Swapnil from the financial planning start-up.

'Amit, can you currently track the investments that you have made for important goals like your children's education and your retirement?'

I wasn't expecting this question. 'No, I do not track my goals. I just track mutual funds as part of my portfolio.'

'Every year, the performance of your fund will change. The fund you selected this year may not work next year and thus your portfolio may need new funds for better returns. Keeping this in mind, how do you rebalance your funds?'

At this point, I was irritated by this questioning. 'I don't do it. The investment process is too manual and time-consuming. I cannot devote so much energy to this exercise. I am constantly travelling.'

'Yes, the manual part of it is painful,' Swapnil agreed. 'But what our algorithms can do is choose the right funds for your important goals and then remind you to rebalance your portfolio in case there are better funds. And all of this is an automated process.'

'What? Is this really possible?' I asked, very surprised at what he was offering.

'Yes, let me show you a demo . . .'

As Swapnil set out to explain what his company was offering, he had no clue that he had wonderfully used Use Case Selling to drive a sale.

Need: Swapnil addressed two unmet needs with respect to my investing exercise; I was aware of one need and unaware of the other. The known need was that I wanted my investments to be more automated so that I would not have to get involved with them on a regular basis. The unknown need was to undertake goal-based investing, an aspect of financial planning that I was not even aware of but appreciated as soon as I was introduced to it.

Insight: I wasn't familiar with the concepts of goal-based investments and automated recommendations.

Conversation/Short Story: In less than three minutes, Swapnil had sparked my interest using pointed questions. His content was relevant and he created a future scenario where my investments were systematic and hassle-free. I was very eager to be a part of the future as compared to the present where I was very unsure of financial planners.

Emotions:

Aspiration: I was excited that finally, I didn't have to make manual investments and that I would get recommendations when I needed them. This would save so much time and ensure a degree of predictability.

Anxiety: I remembered the time and money that was wasted in the past because of poor financial planners. It had been a truly painful experience. Why hadn't I got this solution earlier?

How OnePlus Created a Compelling Brand in a Highly Competitive Cell Phone Market

In 2019, everyone had heard of OnePlus. Now let's go back to 2014 when OnePlus launched their first cell phone in India, which was the OnePlus One. At that point, the market was highly competitive with large players like Apple, Samsung and Sony dominating the landscape. It was almost impossible to imagine that a start-up from China would do well in this situation. Against all odds, OnePlus emerged victorious and created a powerful brand and consistent fan following in the country.

How did they achieve such a feat in the Indian market?

While OnePlus had achieved global appreciation, their rise in India is truly incredible. As per the global research firm Counterpoint, it bagged the top spot with a market share of 40 per cent in India's premium phones segment. It surpassed both Apple and Samsung within five years of its launch. Let's see if the Use Case Selling approach had something to do with this success.

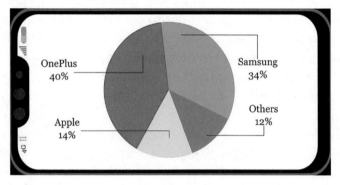

Fig. 5.4[4]

Need: OnePlus satisfied the need of countless users who wanted a high-end cell phone with top-notch features, which looked great but at half the price of the flagship brands. It was priced at Rs 19,999 or $299. The iPhone was launched in India for Rs 53,000 onwards and the Samsung Note 4 was priced at Rs 47,899.

Insight: The fundamental insight that appealed to users like me is that good quality phones are available at reasonable prices. The sandstone finish was the first of its kind that made users believe that holding a high-end phone in their grip is a real pleasure. There was no need for a phone cover because the finish itself was unique and looked great.

Conversation/Story: The brand successfully conveyed its essence through creative taglines. These included 'Never Settle' and '2014 Flagship Killer.'

The tagline 'Never Settle' captured the attention of those who were constantly looking for something bigger and better. They reached out to the people who wanted to challenge the status quo even when it came to phones. Two simple words were packed with power and impact.

OnePlus also positioned their phone as '2014 Flagship Killer'. This one phrase sparked the curiosity and ignited the interest of people who wanted to have flagship phones but couldn't purchase the same because of exorbitant prices. This had such a positive impact that the brand continued the flagship killer strategy for subsequent models.

Emotion: While 'Never Settle' and '2014 Flagship Killer' gave rise to aspiration, the brand's most brilliant move was the novel idea of the *Invite-Only purchase system*. Indian buyers were not at all accustomed to buying phones on an invitation. The system immediately created a mix of anxiety and aspiration among buyers to get their hands on an invite. I remember reaching out to many friends to receive an invitation for buying both OnePlus One and OnePlus Two. And when I got this email, I was absolutely elated before I even had the phone in my hands:

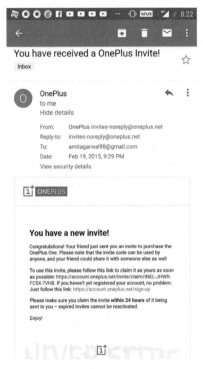

Fig. 5.5

By now, we are getting the hang of detecting the four pillars of Use Case Selling and appreciating the skilful use of this approach in so many famous B2C campaigns. You see how this has been employed by many leading brands to popularize their products and create a niche for themselves in their industries. The success of the OnePlus campaign is another great example of how a strong use case that combines the four pillars in a creative and exciting fashion can work wonders for a brand even when the industry conditions were not suitable for their meteoric rise.

Learning Accelerator: Identify the four NICE pillars of Use Case Selling in this example.

The Successful iPhone Launch in 2007[5]

Steve Jobs was a maverick who gave us many revolutionary products and created the iconic brand Apple. The launch of the iPhone in 2007 is also a great example of the power of Use Case Selling. You will find below a transcribed section of the speech that he made during the launch of the phone.

Jobs: *Well, today, we're introducing three revolutionary products of this class.*

The first is a widescreen iPod with touch controls.
The second is a revolutionary mobile phone.
And the third is a breakthrough Internet communications device.

So, three things: a widescreen iPod with touch controls, a revolutionary mobile phone and a breakthrough Internet communications device.

An iPod, a phone, and an Internet communicator . . . An iPod, a phone; are you getting it?

These are not three separate devices, this is one device, and we are calling it the iPhone.

Today, today, Apple is going to reinvent the phone, and here it is.

No, actually here it is, but we're going to leave it there for now.

Learning Accelerator

This effective checklist will help you identify the elements of Use Case Selling in any given sales situation:

To practise, please fill in the following Use Case Selling checklist for the previous example.

The Four Pillars of Use Case Selling	Y/N	Comments
Need		
Addresses a specific, unserviced need (known need that is not met OR known need that resists change OR unknown need)		
Insights		
Shares valuable information that the customer doesn't know		
Shares valuable information about what other players in the market are doing, including the client success stories, market research and analysis		
Conversation or Short Stories		
Uses questions and/or stories and/or metaphors and/or visuals to involve the user		
Does not involve any technical jargon		
Establishes a contrast to highlight the gap between the existing state and the desired state		
Emotion		
Triggers emotions of aspiration (gain) and/or anxiety(pain)		

Chapter 6

How Use Case Selling Works in Personal Life

'I have always said that everyone is in sales. Maybe you don't hold the title of salesperson but if the business you are in requires you to deal with people, you, my friend, are in sales.'

—Zig Ziglar

All this time, we have been talking about using the Use Case Selling strategy for sales. However, this approach is not of great benefit to sales professionals alone. As a concept, Use Case Selling is equally important and relevant to our personal life. **If a sales professional is selling a product or a service in his or her professional space, we are selling ideas to our family and friends.** Let us study the power of Use Case Selling in our day-to-day lives.

How I Purchased a Rs 10,000 Correspondence Course in 1995

In the year 1995, I was in the second semester of chemical engineering at IIT BHU, Varanasi. While in most cases one had to wait till the end of the first year to get a room in the college hostel, I was fortunate enough to get my own room in the second semester itself. I was absolutely enjoying the space and wanted to use this time to study and learn more. It was during this time that I came across an advertisement in the papers for a diploma in business finance from the Institute of Chartered Financial Analysts of India (ICFAI). I was very interested in the course but my initial excitement vanished when I saw the price. The course fee was Rs 10,000. One can imagine that in 1995, this was a considerable sum. Moreover, my fee for four years of engineering was less than that of the diploma course.

I have always been a person who shares everything with my parents. And even today, I continue to do so. Standing in that phone booth, waiting for the call to connect, I was reluctant and worried about breaking this news.

'Papa, you know that I have always been interested in finance. And earlier, I had considered a career in chartered accountancy. Now, I just came across a diploma course from ICFAI that can be pursued alongside my engineering degree. I think that the exposure from the course will definitely help me during my placements. But the fee is very high. It is Rs 10,000.'

When my father replied, I could sense the pride in his voice. He was happy that his son wanted to learn new things. 'It is good to develop skills in finance while you are studying engineering. It is a bit expensive but we will manage.'

Later, I came to know that he broke his fixed deposits to pay for my course. Of course, this made me very emotional. I felt such gratitude and looking back at this incident, I realize how lucky I've been.

Let's analyse the conversation in the style of Use Case Selling.

Need: My father was the only member of the family employed in the service sector. He knew that I would get a better job during my fourth-year placements if I had good knowledge of something beyond my engineering degree. This was his unmet need. For me, this was an opportunity to study finance as I had once desired to become a chartered accountant.

Insight: My father was happy and proud to know that his son was looking forward to learning something new even while pursuing an engineering degree. He realized that alongside engineering, I was now eager to explore avenues in finance.

Conversation/Short Story: Our conversation over the phone lasted for three to five minutes. We both felt connected.

Emotion: It evoked an emotion of aspiration and growth as my father could sense that I may get a better job due to the additional skills I would acquire via the course.

How Tanish Started Brushing His Teeth Regularly at Night

Like all parents, dental hygiene is of great importance to me. Both my sons have been asked to brush their teeth twice a day, once in the morning and once before bed at night. While my younger one was quick to adopt this habit, his elder brother Tanish took a little more time to understand its importance.

Tanish wasn't too serious at the start and was quite irregular. I tried to approach this topic from various angles. But it was all in vain.

Approach 1: Tanish, please brush your teeth because it keeps your teeth clean.

Approach 2: Tanish, please brush your teeth because your dentist says so.

Approach 3: Tanish, please brush your teeth because your new brush has zig-zag bristles that clean very well.

Approach 4: Tanish, please brush your teeth at night because Aarav does so regularly.

Despite my varied reasoning, nothing seemed to work with Tanish. As a parent, this was worrisome. This was when I came up with a final approach and that made all the difference.

'Tanish, did you happen to watch Virat Kohli's[1] interview after he won the trophy for Man of the Match?'

Tanish enjoys cricket immensely. My words immediately captured his interest.

'Yes Daddy, I did watch the interview. Virat was very happy.'

'And did you see all his photographs in the newspapers and on social media? He was smiling so happily.'

'Yes, he was! My friends even brought a cutout of Virat Kohli to school.'

'Yes, it is a great achievement. Tanish, have you ever wondered what would happen if Virat had unhealthy teeth?'

Tanish wasn't expecting such an odd question. Completely taken aback, he answered quite sadly, 'Daddy, he would look very bad. All the pictures of him smiling would look terrible.'

'This is exactly my point, Tanish! Imagine yourself as a famous cricketer who just became the Man of the Match. Wouldn't it be terrible if all the pictures of you in the papers and on Facebook showed you smiling but with unhealthy, yellow teeth?'

What followed this short conversation was a pleasant change in Tanish's habit. My son immediately went and brushed his teeth. Since that day, I never had to explain the benefits of brushing or constantly remind him to brush twice a day. Tanish follows the given instruction to the T. The image of him victorious, with a trophy in hand, but with yellow teeth was impactful enough to change his habit and take up a healthy one.

Let's identify the Use Case Selling elements in this short conversation.

Need: It addressed Tanish's unfulfilled need to become a famous cricketer. It addressed my known need to improve the dental hygiene of my son but that need was facing some amount of resistance as Tanish was yet to realize the benefits of the same.

Insight: Things that may sound obvious to adults can come as quite a surprise to children. My twelve-year-old son realized that when he became a very famous cricketer, his smile would be seen by so many people across the world. He would be the centre of attention. And if he had to experience all those wonderful things with yellow teeth, it would look quite bad.

Conversation/Short Story: The conversation was short and relevant to my son. Since Tanish loves cricket, he was absorbed. Similarly, I presented a future situation where he was a famous cricketer but with unhealthy teeth. The idea was to bring in a differentiation with respect to the current state.

Emotion

Anxiety: The thought of his favourite cricketer having bad teeth made Tanish anxious. He also realized the repercussions of having bad teeth when he becomes famous.

Aspiration: Tanish imagined himself as a successful cricketer and smiling for the camera. This created a feeling of aspiration.

How My Parents Made Me Buy My Third House

My parents live in Jhansi, a town in north India, and are very happy there. They lead a happy, comfortable life in the presence of relatives and friends. I live in Bangalore, a bustling city in the south, with my wife and children. My parents visit me twice a year but I always wished that they would live with us for longer periods or even consider moving in with us permanently. It is always nice to have the whole family together.

In October 2013, a casual conversation with my parents helped me gain a fresh perspective on why they didn't stay for longer.

I had just returned from work and hot tea was waiting for me. My wife, my parents and I sat in the living room, enjoying a nice evening and some great tea!

'It is so nice to have both of you at home. Why don't you consider living here rather visiting us only twice a year?' I asked my father.

My father's answer and tone quite surprised me. His reply was rather angry.

'Where can we stay comfortably in this house? This is a two-bedroom flat and if we moved in, three people would have to be accommodated in one room. Moreover, our grandchildren are always watching something or the other on the TV. We need a comfortable space to live a happy life, beta. It is not possible in such a scenario.'

For a moment, I didn't know what to say. Never had I imagined this to be the answer. My father's words deeply saddened me. I was completely unaware of the uneasiness my parents felt in my house. This realization, in turn, enabled something that was never on the cards.

What was that? At that point, we were paying the mortgages for two houses simultaneously. Yes, it was stressful but we were managing. Even then I had a word with my wife and we decided to buy a four-bedroom house. We booked the house in 2014 and in April 2018, we moved into the bigger house. My parents were very happy to see a big and spacious house and to have their own, comfortable room. To see such joy on their faces was a wonderful feeling for my wife and me.

During that simple conversation over tea, neither my father nor I knew of the existence of a Use Case Selling structure. Now that I am aware of this strategy, I can easily identify the four pillars of Use Case Selling in this interaction with my parents. In a short conversation that lasted for two to four minutes, my father shared his experience. He told us about an unmet need and the pain associated with the same. The discomfort he felt in my home came as an insight to my wife and me, albeit an unpleasant one. I felt anxious and this propelled us to buy a third house.

How I Finally Convinced My Wife to 'Crush the Debt'

By the grace of God, the blessings of my parents and the support of a loving family, I have done very well professionally and have been earning well. But when your earnings increase, expenses increase. And my biggest expenses were the multiple mortgages. At one point, we were paying off six mortgages. Yes, you read it correctly . . . six! With time, we closed four of them and were left with two loans, amounting to Rs 1,20,000 in mortgage payments (equated monthly instalments or EMIs). These EMIs created a lot of pressure on me and were holding me back from starting something on my own. So, while life appeared to be quite rosy on the outside, internally, the stress of mortgages was a constant source of worry and was always at the back of my mind.

My wife and I had always thought of selling one of our three properties if the need arose. But we never got around to discussing it thoroughly and kept waiting for the right time. And the right time never seemed to come. It was only in 2018 that I read two books that shook me to take action with respect to my loans. *Awaken the Millionaire* and *Zero Debt* both spoke of the urgency to 'crush your debts'. In *Zero Debt*, the author had to be admitted to the ICU under the crippling pressure of his eight loans! I did not want to be in that terrible position. I surely didn't want to go through what the author did. I decided to take up the issue of our loans with Ashi, my wife, and come to a solid solution, once and for all.

After breakfast, I asked my wife if she recollected the loan amount we took to purchase our house in Hyderabad.

'Yes, we took forty lakh[2] in 2009,' she said.

That's correct. Now I recently found out that in the last nine years, we have paid Rs 45 lakh to the bank and yet we have an outstanding amount of Rs 25 lakh left to pay up! And not only that, this means that we have paid Rs 15 lakh as principal and Rs 30 lakh as interest!'

Ashi was shocked at this revelation. Her eyes were wide open.

'What? I cannot believe this, Amit. We still have to pay 25 lakh?'

'Yes, Ashi,' I answered quite sadly. '25 lakh to go.'

Quite naturally, my wife and I were distressed, but now we knew that we just had to sell one of our houses.

The one in Hyderabad was the most obvious choice and we went ahead with it.

So what was the difference in my approach this time as opposed to my previous attempts when we did not discuss it as seriously as we should have?

I visualized Ashi as a potential buyer. I was the sales owner who knew that selling off the property was the best solution and therefore, had to convince her of the same. And as a sales owner, I obviously used Use Case Selling.

Need: There were two needs in this scenario; a known need that was facing resistance and an unknown need. The former was the fact that we had to close our loans but we didn't move ahead with it. The latter was that we had paid Rs 15,00,000 as principal and Rs 30,00,000 as interest.

Insight: After nine years, we had only paid Rs 15,00,000 as the principal in spite of paying Rs 45,00,000 to the bank. It was quite a painful realization.

Conversation/Short Story: It was a short conversation that went on for three minutes.

Emotion: The insight caused anxiety, sadness and a strong sense of loss in both of us. This feeling was in line with the loss aversion theory we covered in chapter 2.

How My Sons Decided Not to Eat Out Every Week

My sons, like most children, love eating out. Every weekend, after a game of football at a sports facility, we enjoy breakfast there. On a regular Saturday morning, after a great game, we finished a hearty meal of lovely dosas and fresh juice. I asked for the bill and the amount was Rs 540. Now, breakfast at the Play Arena every Saturday and Sunday was an old practice. I never really gave it much thought. But that day, I decided to discuss the bill with my sons.

'Tanish, do you know how much I paid for today's breakfast?'

'No Daddy, how much?' he inquired.

'Today's bill amount is Rs 540. And how many days a month do we eat breakfast here?'

'Since we come here every weekend, it would mean ten days a month.'

'Great; now can you tell me how much we would be spending every month?'

'Daddy, that amount will be Rs 540 multiplied by 10. We spend Rs 5400 monthly.'

'So can you calculate and let me know how much we are spending on breakfast every year?'

Although Tanish was yet to understand the purpose of the discussion, he was enjoying the process as both my sons are quite fond of math. He calculated the amount and it was Rs 64,800. And of course, he was surprised!

'What do you think of this amount, Tanish?' I asked him.

'Daddy, Rs 64,800 on breakfast is too much!' he exclaimed, with wide open eyes.

Such was the impact of that simple calculation that he even shared the same with his brother and mother. In the past, I tried to use logic such as eating out too often is not healthy and very expensive. But it didn't seem to have much of an effect. Use Case Selling worked. Why?

Need: It fulfilled my known need for inculcating fiscal discipline within the family, which had previously faced high levels of resistance.

Insight: Both Tanish and I were surprised that we were spending Rs 64,800 per year for breakfast just over the weekend. Taking the 30 per cent tax bracket into account, this translates to a pre-tax income worth Rs 92,571. This is a lot of money for breakfast over the weekend.

Conversation/Short Story: The conversation lasted for three minutes and Tanish was completely involved. He enjoys math and calculating the bill amount was of interest to him.

Emotion: 'It's too much, Daddy'; Tanish was surprised and anxious.

As you can see, Use Case Selling has helped me navigate through many difficult situations in my personal life. Sometimes, our loved ones need a little more clarity before they can take a decision. We could gently guide them through that. And the best part is that the four pillars of Use Case Selling always surround us. There is always scope for discovering an unserviced need, sharing insights, engaging in conversation and evoking an emotion. It is up to us to identify them and use them well. It is sure to click!

Learning Accelerator: Try and identify the four NICE pillars of Use Case Selling in this example.

Can I Get One Year Extra Every 4 Four Years?

Sometimes, a single moment can transform your lifestyle for the better and the Bollywood superstar Akshay Kumar was instrumental in helping my family create such a moment. It was a usual Sunday and my sons were making the most of it. They had enjoyed a game of football in the morning, followed by some family time with their cousin and then a birthday of a close friend in the afternoon. I went to pick them up at 4 p.m. and as I waited for them to come down to the car, I watched   a video[3] where Akshay Kumar shared three indispensable lifestyle changes that one needs to inculcate to ensure great health throughout your life. These were:

1. Waking up at 4 a.m.
2. Exercising for an hour daily
3. Not eating after 6.30 p.m. (sunset)

As I was reflecting on the video and the three lessons, Tanish and Aarav arrived and we headed home. My sons were beaming with joy. They had had a wonderful time at the party. I took advantage of the happy atmosphere and asked them to watch the video. After they were done, we started discussing the advice given by Akshay Kumar in the video.

'Guys, when do you wake up every morning?' I asked my sons.

'6.30 a.m.,' both answered.

'And what time do your friends wake up?'

'Around the same time as us.'

'Kids, Akshay Kumar wakes up at 4 a.m. every morning. He says that he doesn't remember a day when he hasn't seen the sunrise. Right now, 4 a.m. is too much to aspire for. So if we try to start our day at 5 a.m. instead of 6.30 a.m., how much time will we gain?'

'One and a half hours more every day, Daddy,' both my sons answered.

'Excellent,' I said. 'But that is just the amount of time you gain in a day. Why don't we calculate the time we gain in one month?'

'Daddy, in one month we will gain 1.5 hours into thirty days, which is forty-five hours!' Tanish answered.

'That is absolutely correct! And what about the time we get in a year? You see, forty-five hours per month means 540 extra hours in a year,' I said.

By now, Tanish and Aarav were listening with rapt attention. I continued.

'And in four years, this will equal 2160 extra hours. In a day there are eight working hours. Assuming twenty-two working days in a month, we work 2112 hours in a year. That means you will get one additional year extra every four years if you wake up at 5 a.m. every day.'

My sons were spellbound. Both of them were excited, speechless and very, very surprised. What followed next was more surprising . . .

Both Tanish and Aarav asked me to wake them up at 5 a.m. Parents know how children like to copy each other. But there was something different about their resolve.

I was very happy to see their reaction. I told them we could start from the following morning as they had a long day and also because Monday, 3 September was a school holiday. In the morning, they both shared this with their mother with a lot of excitement. Their mother was also astonished.

In the evening, both kids had brushed their teeth and we were about to go to bed when Aarav said, with an innocent smile, 'Daddy, please wake me up at 5 a.m.'

My nine-year-old son saying this with so much innocence and conviction!

I couldn't have asked for more. I was a bit emotional and I said, 'I will wake you both up. Good night, guys!'

On 4 September, I started waking them up at 5.11 a.m. and they both were awake at 5.30 a.m.

What followed next was one of the most memorable mornings for us as a family.

We first did drawing and reading and then went to our terrace to see the sunrise and enjoy nature.

Enjoying the sunrise

Then we went cycling.

Off on a cycle tour

We live in the suburbs of Bangalore, near farmlands. Enjoying the clouds, sunrise, birds chirping on the terrace and farmlands while cycling was a memorable experience.

This all happened because a nine-year-old and a twelve-year-old believed that they could get one year extra every four years if they woke up at 5 a.m.

Learning Accelerator

This effective checklist will help you identify the Use Case Selling elements in any given sales situation.

To practise, please fill in the following Use Case Selling checklist for the previous example.

The Four Pillars of Use Case Selling	Y/N	Comments
Need		
Addresses a specific, unserviced need (known need that is not met OR known need that resists change OR unknown need)		
Insights		
Shares valuable information that the customer doesn't know		
Shares valuable information about what other players in the market are doing, including the client success stories, market research and analysis		
Conversation or Short Stories		
Uses questions and/or stories and/or metaphors and/or visuals to involve the user		
Does not involve any technical jargon		
Establishes a contrast to highlight the gap between the existing state and the desired state		
Emotion		
Triggers emotions of aspiration (gain) and/or anxiety(pain)		

The sixteen examples narrated in chapters 4, 5 and 6 would have surely deepened your understanding of the four NICE pillars of Use Case Selling. Now can you go to the Learning Accelerator in Chapter 1 and double-check it using the checklist above?

Chapter 7

Why Is Use Case Selling So Effective?

'The human mind is the ultimate sales machine because it is constantly generating countless thoughts and most of these finally lead up to selling an idea'

—Amit Agarwal

In the last three chapters, we saw various examples of Use Case Selling in both our professional and personal lives. In all cases, it has worked very effectively. While carefully studying the examples hitherto, through the four pillars of Use Case Selling, a few questions may have crossed your mind. **Why does Use Case Selling work? Is there a science to it? Does our brain have an answer?** Let's see if we can answer them.

The human brain has three parts[1] and each part **is responsible for a specific set of functions:**

Rational (logic, data and figures)

Emotional (memories, feelings and experiences)

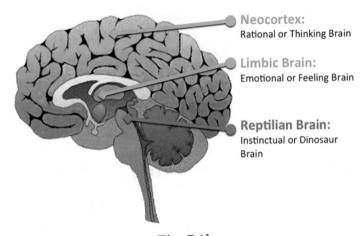

Fig. 7.1[2]

Reptilian (instant decision-making, fight or flight syndrome)

Rational Brain (the neocortex): This part of the brain was the latest to develop in the course of evolution. Thus, it is often called the 'new brain'. It is responsible for processing rational elements such as facts, data, language, logical skills and analytical skills. *When we use data, logic and facts, we are speaking to the rational brain.*

Emotional Brain (limbic brain): This portion is called the 'old brain'. It supports various functions including social interactions, emotions, behaviour and memory. It is basically the repository of human emotions and feelings. *When we use our emotions, we are talking to the emotional brain.*

Reptilian Brain: This is the oldest structure of our brain. Because of our reptilian origins, this part of the brain is very instinctive and fast. It is responsible for our safety, sensing and avoiding possible dangers, and survival instincts (fight or flight). *While deciding, the reptilian brain asks, 'What's in it for me? Is there danger?'*

An example will help you understand how the three parts work. After a very tiring day at work and struggling with the Bangalore traffic, I reached home. I was exhausted and was looking forward to a hot cup of tea. My wife decided to make me some ginger tea. At that point, I was very happy. I felt that this was exactly what I needed to soothe myself (emotional brain). As I was awaiting my tea, I suddenly remembered that I was on medication. My doctor had advised me to avoid caffeinated beverages (rational brain). I should have stopped Ashi from making the tea but in the past, a cup of hot tea has helped me unwind and I believe that tea is always a great relaxant (emotional brain, again). But unfortunately, I did not realize how hot it was. As soon as I sipped it, my tongue got burnt and I had to spit it out (reptilian brain).

Just as the different parts of the brain respond to day-to-day situations, they react differentially to the four pillars of Use Case Selling. Each pillar contains within itself certain triggers that immediately connect a particular part of the brain and the use case structure.

Use Case Structure	Part of the Brain	Triggers That Connect Parts of the Brain and Use Case Structures
Need	Reptilian brain	What's in it for me as a customer?
Insight	Emotional brain and rational brain	Having a mix of emotions, data and logic
Conversation or Story	Emotional brain	Use of visuals Creating the contrast Use of metaphor
Emotion	Emotional brain and reptilian brain	Giving rise to emotions of aspiration and anxiety. Anxiety appeals to the reptilian brain

Now, I have another question. *When it comes to making decisions, which part of the brain exercises the greatest control over the process?* To address this query, we will consider the following situations:

Why do we say, 'I have a gut feeling that this idea will work out'?

A gut feeling is always attached to your memories, emotions and past experiences.

Why do we say 'Listen to your heart' rather than 'Listen to your mind'?
The heart is associated with our emotions and our mind is connected with logic.

Why do brands use celebrities to endorse their products?
Have you noticed that many popular brands have famous celebrities advertising their products? We've seen Lionel Messi advertising the Tiago car and Sachin Tendulkar as an ambassador for a popular energy drink.

Fig. 7.2[3]

Now, what if Tiago decided to sell its car by simply stating the features and not involving Messi? Imagine an advertisement for the popular energy drink without Sachin Tendulkar endorsing it. Will these campaigns create an iota of impact on the consumer in you? Unfortunately, they won't! Even though these are great products, why aren't they sold using their features and benefits? **This happens because features and benefits do not have an emotional quotient.** They give out information in a rather straightforward and unappealing way. On the other hand, brand ambassadors create an emotion of aspiration in buyers like us. We want to use the products that our heroes are using. Thus, they appeal to the consumer.

Aristotle's Key Persuasion: Ethos, Logos and Pathos

I have mentioned earlier how the Greek philosopher Aristotle identified three modes of persuasion: Ethos, Logos and Pathos. Just to quickly recap . . .

Ethos: Highlighting the credibility of a presenter
Logos: Use of logic, data, facts, figures, statistics, etc.
Pathos: Appeals to the emotions of the crowd (sympathy, anger, vulnerability, aspiration, anxiety)

In the past few years, TED Talks have become very popular. It is a global platform bringing together heroes from all over the world who have some truly inspirational stories to tell about their lives, overcoming odds and their interesting and phenomenal work in so many fields. Carmine Gallo, the author of *Talk like Ted*, studied the most successful TED Talks. He came to an excellent and highly relevant conclusion[4] that the most successful TED Talks are based on:

65 per cent Pathos
25 per cent Logos
10 per cent Ethos

Pathos appeals to our emotional brain.

What Happens If the Emotional Part of the Brain Is Damaged?

The famous neuroscientist Antonio Damasio conducted an in-depth study on the lives of individuals who experienced some damage to the emotional part of their brain.[5, 6] His patient, Elliott, was leading the perfect life; he had a great career and a loving family. Unfortunately, he had to undergo surgery for the removal of the part of the brain that regulates emotion. Following the surgery, his life took an unexpected turn. Elliott reported to Damasio that even the simplest of actions took too much time and effort. While it may surprise you to note that Elliott's intellect remained absolutely normal, it took him half an hour to make an appointment and even longer to choose a pen to fill out a form. Imagine yourself to be in a position where deciding where to eat lunch becomes so exhausting and time-consuming that it seems like an actual chore. It was then that Damasio realized that Elliott's lack of emotions made him incapable of taking the simplest of decisions. We can conclude that **emotions are the key to making decisions.**

If our emotional quotient is instrumental in decision-making, then the following statements must hold true:

- A bad use case will not appeal to the emotional part of the brain at all.
- A very good use case will appeal only to the emotional part of the brain by creating emotions.
- A brilliant use case will appeal to all three parts of the brain by giving rise to myriad emotions, making prudent use of data and highlighting what's in it for the buyer with utmost clarity.

With these pointers in mind, I thought of testing out this theory. And one morning, I found a great chance to do so. As my wife had stopped drinking tea, I began to miss the old times when we enjoyed a cup together. On a particularly cold morning in Bangalore, my craving for a hot cuppa with my wife became quite strong. I decided to give it a shot.

'Ashi, it is quite cold today, isn't it?' I asked her.

'Yes, it is,' Ashi agreed.

'Ashi, remember winters in Jhansi when we used to talk for hours over cups of warm and comforting ginger tea? This cold weather makes me want to relive those memories and talk leisurely over tea. I am making a cup for myself. Should I make some for you as well?'

Ashi smiled lovingly. 'Yes, I remember those days in Jhansi. I wouldn't mind half a cup today.'

Needless to say, I was absolutely thrilled and we enjoyed a wonderful morning. And I owe this success to the power of Use Case Selling that appealed to the emotional part of the brain. What would have happened if

I had approached this topic differently? Maybe something like this:

'Ashi, why don't you drink some tea today?' Or 'Would you like to drink a cup of tea just for today?'

'No dear, you know I have stopped drinking tea.'

And this would have been the end of the conversation. Thus appealing to the emotional brain is critical for utilizing the true power of Use Case Selling.

Learning Accelerator

Now that we have understood the importance of emotions, what scenarios come to your mind wherein you or someone you have interacted with has used emotion to convey a need?

_____

_____

_____

_____

_____

_____

_____

_____

_____

_____

_____

_____

_____

_____

Chapter 8

What Are the Five Mindsets That Can Fuel Excellence in Use Case Selling?

'Whether you think you can, or you think you can't—you're right'
—Henry Ford

As evident from the examples in the B2B, B2C and personal spheres, Use Case Selling's four NICE pillars structure is easy, effective and can be replicated. When a sales owner follows this structure, success becomes predictable. Till now, we have studied several examples and identified the need, insight, conversation or the short story and the emotion involved. This chapter takes Use Case Selling a step further. To help a sales owner, we will now talk about the mindsets that can expedite your journey of excellence in Use Case Selling.

I have identified five mindsets.

Mindset 1: Thought Leader Mindset

Have you faced a situation where you asked a sales owner a question and he or she brings in an expert or a supervisor to address your query? As a customer, how do you feel when this happens? Not good, isn't it?

As opposed to this situation, imagine a presentation where you interact with a sales owner who:

- Has a deep understanding of product/space
- Has a deep understanding of client business
- Is extremely persuasive in written and verbal communication

How would you feel then? There is a high chance that after the presentation, you will say, 'This person is an expert. He is a thought leader.'

This transformation from a salesperson to a thought leader is a two-step process.

Step 1—Intention

> *'Our intention creates our reality'*
> —Wayne Dyer

Quite often, sales owners depend on product specialists and technical specialists to assist them in client interaction. This happens partly because of the organizational structure and partly due to the sales owner's individual approach. And it is exactly this personal approach that needs to be transformed from being hesitant and dependent to becoming proactive and positive. The following positive affirmations or declarations can be used to develop the thought leader inside you. Consider this:

I am a thought leader in < name of space that you are selling > (for example, I am a thought leader in digital transformation).

I continuously share insights that my clients find valuable.

The above declarations, when repeated regularly, create a strong intention that fuels the transition to a thought leader. Repeat such declarations to yourself as often as possible. This will go a long way in reaffirming your belief in what you do and will help your attitude in sales to develop in the right direction.

Step 2—Action

In addition to strengthening your intentions to become a thought leader, there are some action-oriented frameworks that will help this transition.

PPF (PAST, PRESENT AND FUTURE)

Think about this. A thought leader in any field of work will always have views about the past, present and future of the zone he works for. The PPF framework makes use of elements such as success stories, capabilities and extensive learning gained from experience over a vast period of time.

Let's take an example. Since I head sales, many companies reach out to me for selling different software, including customer relationship management (CRM). Now say, Scott, a sales owner, reaches out to me to pitch HubSpot. HubSpot happens to be a famous CRM software in the

B2B space. Scott uses the PPF framework to prepare for a discussion with me.

Past	Please share, in detail, your top three success stories regarding the use of HubSpot in India.
Present	Among all of HubSpot's CRM capabilities, which 20 per cent create 80 per cent of value for clients?
Future	What are the top five trends in the CRM space in the next one to three years? How is HubSpot planning to address them?

Assuming that Scott answers my questions accurately and confidently, what kind of impression will he create in my mind? I would think, 'Scott is wonderful. He knows his clients, the product and the CRM space.'

As in the case of CRM, following this simple structure can be used as a great template to increase knowledge in any area of functioning or interest:

Past	Please share in detail your top three success stories regarding the usage of <product name>
Present	Among all of <product name's > capabilities, which 20 per cent creates 80 per cent of value for clients?
Future	What are the top five trends in <area of work> in the next one to three years? How is <company name> planning to address them?

An even more comprehensive framework will look like this:

Past	Please share in detail your top 3 success stories regarding the usage of <product name>
	How has your value proposition evolved over the last five years?
	What have been your top three failures/challenges in serving clients post the sale?
Present	Among all of <product name's > capabilities, which 20 per cent creates 80 per cent of value for clients?
	What are the top three requirements that clients are currently asking for, which you cannot support them on as yet?
Future	What are the top five trends in <area of work> in the next one to three years? How is <company> planning to address them?

MOST–FEW–NONE

This framework creates an easy structure to cover two aspects related to the insights pillar of Use Case Selling. These are 'Tell me something I don't know' and 'Tell me what others are doing'. Let's illustrate this with an example. Let's say I have to present my view on lead generation using the Most–Few–None framework.

What lead generation capabilities do most B2B companies use for lead generation?

Answer: Database preparation, outbound cold calling, website lead forms and email campaigns.

What lead generation capabilities do a few B2B companies use for lead generation?
Answer: Database refresh and synch up with LinkedIn, account-based marketing (ABM), intent data and social selling.

What lead generation capabilities do none/very few of the B2B companies use for lead generation?
Answer: Video for prospecting, automating connection requests on LinkedIn and automating personalized messages on LinkedIn.

As you can see, the above information can be represented very concisely. If required, each topic can be explained separately. Now if we only keep the first sentence intact (the most statement) and delete the remaining two (the few and none statements), will it create the same impact? No, it won't. It is the amazing combination of Most–Few–None that offers a clear contrast and makes the pitch click.

The same framework can be extended to personal situations. When I moved to Bangalore in 2010, my wife and I had to search for a new school for Tanish. I visited about ten to twelve schools before taking the call. Now let's use the Most–Few–None framework to analyse the selection of the school.

Among the ten to twelve schools that I visited:

What facilities are most schools providing for the holistic development of the child?

Answer: Activities, play facilities, good teachers, multimedia facilities and laboratories.

What facilities are few schools providing for the holistic development of the child?
Answer: Montessori style of experiential education, higher teacher-to-child ratio (1:15).

What facilities are none of the schools providing for the holistic development of the child?
Answer: Spiritual development.

In the end, we chose Sri Sri Ravi Shankar Vidya Mandir (SSRVM). This was the only school that addressed spiritual development in addition to providing all the other amenities that the remaining schools were.

Become a Trusted Adviser using one simple framework:

MOST–FEW–NONE

Scan the QR code to watch the video

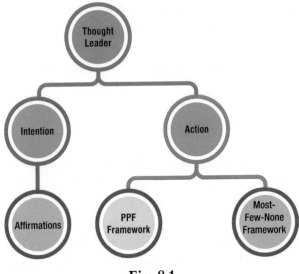

Fig. 8.1

Mindset 2: Service Mindset

Clint Eastwood's words beautifully summarize the essence of the service mindset. He said, 'It's not about you. It's about them.'

It is so simple to read and yet difficult to implement. Let's consider the following scenario to understand the subtle nuances of the service mindset.

A software company called FGH Systems implemented their customer experience software for ABC Bank over a period of six months. This increased customer acquisition by 30 per cent. FGH Systems now wants to launch a press release to share the story of their successful implementation. What could be a good headline for this press release?

ABC Bank increases customer acquisition by 30 per cent using user-level personalization.

OR

FGH System helps ABC Bank to increase their customer acquisition by 30 per cent using its proprietary algorithms for user-level personalization

At first glance, both these headlines may appear to be fairly regular. Now, the question is, *which headline demonstrates the service mindset?*

In the first headline, the customer is your hero. They are at the forefront. In the second headline, the solution provider is the hero. Clearly, the first headline exhibits the service mindset because the centre of focus is the benefit of the customers.

So how do we understand the needs of the customers in order to put them at the forefront?

Quite naturally, one of the most effective ways to develop the customer-first, service mindset is to understand which of the client's unserviced requirements could be fulfilled. A very effective way of understanding this is to work on the customer's Unique Buying Point rather than blindly following the old tradition of the Unique Selling Point. The term Unique Selling Point (USP) has been a catchphrase in marketing for many decades. But the question is, *is the concept of USP organization-centric or customer-centric?* The Unique Selling Proposition or the Unique Selling Point is clearly more focused on differentiation with competition rather than the customer.

In stark contrast, the Unique Pain Point (UPP) refers to the specific, unserviced need of the customer. Once the customers are made aware of various UPPs, it becomes their Unique Buying Proposition (UBP). Use Case Selling focuses on identifying the unserviced needs of the customers rather than the USP of the product. The UPP naturally progresses into a UBP.

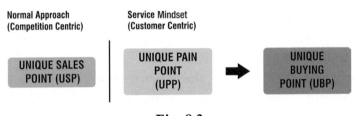

Fig. 8.2

Mahatma Gandhi summarized the importance of a service mindset in his famous quote:

'*A customer is the most important visitor on our premises. He is not dependent on us. We are dependent on him. He is not an interruption in our work. He is the purpose of it. He is not an outsider in our business. He is part of it. We are not doing him a favour by serving him. He is doing us a favour by giving us an opportunity to do so.*'

The following questions can help us assess and cultivate the service mindset within the organization:

Who is the hero of the success story?

Whose promotion are we working towards?

What success metrics are we tracking and presenting to our clients on a monthly/quarterly/annual basis?

How could we help our clients in the next <x> months so that they win a coveted award next year?

Mindset 3: Challenging the Status Quo Mindset

'Anybody who gets upset and/or expects you to say YES all of the time clearly doesn't have your best interest at heart'
—Stephanie Lahart

Have you come across a sales owner who agrees to everything their client says, even though they don't agree with it or feel it is not good for the customer? This may happen because of their respect for the client or the fear of losing the client. The ability to politely challenge the status quo and offer alternative options to help your clients is essential to develop trust with them. This will help them make informed decisions, will sharpen your skills and increase your credibility in the eyes of your clients. Let's look at the following true scenarios.

I met Krishnan, SVP IT, HR and procurement for a large bank in Asia. My team had already been in touch with the bank for around twelve months and the meeting that I attended was supposed to be a closure meeting. After exchanging pleasantries, Krishnan started the conversation on a rather stiff note.

'Mr Agarwal, your company's proposal is very strange. Your price is three times higher than other vendors in this space. At the same time, you take twice the time to implement the software. I have never heard of anything like this.'

At that moment, I was caught up with preparing the PowerPoint presentation and slides that contained all the relevant data. Naturally, I was quite surprised by Krishnan's straightforward approach and blunt words right at the start of the meeting. For a minute, I felt that he wasn't satisfied with us and that we may not win this account. Nonetheless, the situation required me to gain composure.

'Thank you for your feedback, Mr Krishnan. We made this software live in twelve banks. The projected slide has the name of the bank, the reports and the time taken for its implementation. So, based on our extensive experience while working with them and the data we have collected, we believe it will take five months to implement this software in your bank. I personally encourage innovation in everything. While it is difficult for me to say this, if you find any other partner that can implement this software with the same quality, in less time and at a lower cost, I would advise you to go with them. I would have done the same.'

And do you know what happened next? We got the order! Constructively challenging the conventional stream of thought always helps. The same can help you in your personal life as well.

A friend of mine is an engineer from the prestigious IIT Kharagpur. However, his true passion lay in psychology. That was his inner calling. Therefore, he decided to join a course to pursue the subject. He called the university to apply for this course despite the fact that the admissions deadline was over. He even got in touch with a university representative who told him, 'No, you are well past the application dates.' For most, this would be a no-brainer situation. It would mean time to look for another institution. But what my friend said was so wonderfully unexpected.

He said, 'All right. But ten years from now, there is a very high chance that you will regret not letting a legend in psychology attend your university because he missed out on a deadline.'

And interestingly, he got admission to the course. Such a fascinating incident!

Mindset 4: Storytelling Mindset

A quality that comes naturally to sales owners is asking questions. This is because the efficacy of questioning in sales has been stressed for many years now.

On the other hand, storytelling from the context of sales is a fresh approach and thus, requires more effort. In addition to formal training, the following techniques will help you develop a storyteller's mindset and strengthen your capabilities to express and show your stories.

Conduct a client meeting without using physical props, demos or PowerPoint presentations. I have often noticed that when I speak to a client without such tools to aid me, it created more credibility in the eyes of the client. Of course, such an approach requires thorough preparation.

One has to make good use of tonality, gestures and the whiteboard to create an interesting environment.

We all must be familiar with the concept of TED Talks. The success of a TED Talk not only depends on the strength of the story being told but also the charisma of the speaker and his or her ability to create an atmosphere. Now, watch the following TED Talks very closely:

How to speak so that people want to listen by Julian Treasure[1]

How great leaders inspire action by Simon Sinek[2]

The Unheard Story of David and Goliath by Malcolm Gladwell[3]

After carefully watching these videos, answer each of the following questions for each of the TED Talks:

The top three things that you liked about them.

Does the speaker use an element of contrast?

Is the language used simple to understand?

Does the speaker use any metaphors? If yes, mention the same.

Does the speaker ask any questions? If yes, mention the same.

List instances where the speaker uses the following tools:

Visuals

Tonality

Gesture

The idea is to study how they conduct the TED Talks. So once in six or twelve months, deliver a TED Talk-like speech in less than eighteen minutes about your product, service or idea. This could be one of the exercises in the sales team offsite. If it is not possible as a group activity, videotape your speech and then review it alone or with others.

If possible, try to engage your children/relatives in storytelling. I have two sons and I used to tell them stories almost every night. Now you may ask me where I found so many stories to tell them. Did I repeat the stories? No, I could not repeat those! And why is that? Because kids are very sharp! The second I tried telling them a story they had heard before, they would figure it out, stop me and say, 'No, Daddy. We want a new story.' Initially, it was slightly tough to think of a fresh story every night. But then I started creating stories on the go. And honestly, I started enjoying the process of coming up with new plots, characters and scenes every night. I think my use of gestures, tonality and my tendency to create a very vivid, visual description of things in these stories tremendously helped me in business. All it required was daily practice in the form of two bedtime stories.

Consider joining a public speaking club, or something along those lines, near your area. Have you noticed that many successful public speakers use stories to make their point? Why does it happen? The answer lies in a research conducted by the London Business School which suggests that people retain 65 to 70 per cent of the information shared through stories, while only 5 to 10 per cent of information is retained through the dry presentation of data and statistics.[4] So a good speaker will use stories because people remember stories. An ecosystem like a public speaking club provides an opportunity to polish speaking skills. If one has to present a short speech ranging from one to six minutes every week, his or her speaking prowess will witness manifold improvement.

Mindset 5: Unearthing New Needs

The first pillar of Use Case Selling is to identify an unserviced need. Can an ethical sale happen without us being aware of the real need that needs to be serviced? No, it cannot happen. The key to the sale lies in addressing that point of concern of the customer that is yet to come across a solution. While the product's research and development wing will be actively involved in unearthing such unserviced needs, sales owners can identify the same in the following ways:

Creating a Handy Repository of Needs of the Top Five Customers

Knowing which needs are being addressed increases the knowledge and confidence of a sales owner. Instead of using fancy case studies, a simple template like this will be more effective:

S. No.	Client Name	Country	Need Description	Need Category	Product/Service Capability That is Solving the Need	Benefits

Asking the Correct Questions at Every Level

There are a number of levels at play when it comes to sales. You have the larger organization, members of the sales team and the clients. And at each level, the correct questions will give rise to the correct answers that positively contribute to making the sale.

Questions for the Larger Organization

There are two questions that will really help an organization to understand the needs of their customers that are yet to be serviced. They are as follows:

1. What are the top five needs that are currently not on our roadmap but will create maximum impact for our clients?
2. What are the top five needs that our competitors are addressing and we are not?

Questions for the Clients

Once the context is set and a rapport is built with the client, I have found these questions can be very effective:

1. Among the various use cases that I have shared with you, which are the top three cases that created the most value for you? Whenever I ask this question, I have found a sense of prioritization arising within the client. This creates an immediate buy-in.
2. It is great to see you have <bring in the achievement of your client>. Is there any requirement that is still not met and is in line with your vision of being the best in <specific area>?
3. I have shared a number of success stories. Thank you for your appreciation. Is there is any requirement that you have that I may not have covered?

4. Assuming that budget and approvals are not an issue, which is the one unmet need that you would want to address?

Questions for Other Sales Members

Sales teams are spread over many countries and geographical regions. A requirement handled by one sales owner is completely new for other sales owners.

What are the top three unmet needs in <area> for <industry name> clients in <country/region>?

For example: What are the top three unmet needs in predictive analytics for retail clients in Indonesia?

Market Feedback

In addition to these questions, keeping in touch with market updates through channels such as clients, partners, competitors, regulators and technology trends can be extremely useful in identifying new requirements.

Let's study an example of how hearing about a regulatory change can transform the strategy of an entire company. In October 2010, a sales owner from my team came across an important paper by the Reserve Bank of India. This paper contained guidelines for all banks requiring them to submit their regulatory reports in an automated manner and by a specific date. He shared the paper with me and I then discussed the same with my CEO and other executives.

After due diligence and many discussions, this paper resulted in the company pivoting from being an analytics company to regulatory compliance. In the Mount Everest of the needs model, this requirement of automating regulatory reports was largely unknown to banks before RBI released the document in 2010. So in this case, listening to market updates helped in changing the strategy of the company. It happened only because a diligent sales owner was aware of the happenings of the market.

Here's a template that could be useful while keeping up with market updates:

S. No.	Source Type	Source Name	Trend/ Need Description	Need Category	Product/ Service Capability that is Solving It	Comments

Learning Accelerator

1. Stories are based on our experiences. If you had to choose three experiences from your personal or professional life that could be made into compelling stories that would move people, what would they be?

Experience 1 _____

_____

_____

Experience 2 _____

_____

_____

Experience 3 _____

_____

_____

Experience 4 _____

_____

_____

2. Think of a product, service or idea that you want to sell; what are the 'Most–Few–None' criteria you could include in your pitch, to your advantage?

Most _____

_____

_____

Few _____

_____

_____

None _____

_____

_____

3. Now think of one product, service or idea that you want to buy; what are the 'Most–Few–None' criteria that you would use while shortlisting and eliminating options?

Most _____

_____

_____

Few _____

_____

_____

None _____

_____

_____

4.   What are the key elements of a service mindset?

☐   Customer is the hero
☐   Seller (vendor) is the hero
☐   Identify customer value metrics upfront

Chapter 9

What Are the Three Tools That Can Fuel Excellence in Use Case Selling?

'Between selling a product, service or idea, selling an idea is the most difficult because an idea is not tangible'
—Amit Agarwal

In the previous chapter, we discussed five mindsets that one would need to inculcate to achieve excellence in Use Case Selling. Now let's discuss a few tools that gel very well with such mindsets and are sure to give you even better results. These three tools beautifully complement the five mindsets and the result of this synergy is brilliance in Use Case Selling. These three tools are:

1. Rapport

What happens when you meet somebody from your city?
What happens when someone shares a story that you absolutely relate to?

What happens when someone inspires you to become something great in the future?
What happens when you receive genuine praise and appreciation from someone?

In each of the four situations, we feel an immediate liking and sense of connection with the other person. Why is that so? This is because all these questions are either establishing a similarity or conferring praise. The first three highlight a similarity between a person and you. The last question highlights the praise factor. *So praise and similarity are key factors in building an immediate rapport.*

Let's analyse certain ways of exploring similarity and praise to develop a rapport:

Show Me That You Know Me

Social media platforms and the Internet provide great opportunities to conduct research about the person or organization of interest. If you can acquaint yourself with their interests, you could leverage these as a great conversation starter.

Here are some examples of how your 'research' can be put to use.

You could mention, 'I noticed on LinkedIn that you went to IIT Kanpur for engineering. It is so nice to meet a college senior.'

Or you could say, 'I really enjoyed your interview on employee empowerment. Your views on working from home can really help create an inclusive environment.'

Physical Mirroring and Matching

This is a very simple method because it creates a similarity by just copying the physical movement of others. If somebody has crossed their legs, gently cross yours. If somebody is raising the right hand while they speak, you do the same.

But what is the difference between matching and mirroring while copying movements?

In matching, you replicate the exact physical movements. In mirroring, you match the exact physical movement utilizing the other side.

Matching: If somebody raises his right hand, you raise your right hand.

Mirroring: If somebody raises his right hand, you raise your left hand.

This technique works like magic when you are interacting with people of diverse cultural backgrounds. For this, we don't need to prepare in advance. We just need to be aware and match the actions, subtly.

Matching Tonality and Words

I have a rather interesting example related to matching tonality and words. Consider two people in love. The man confesses his love and says, 'I love you, honey.' The woman reciprocates and says, 'I love you too, my dear.'

What is common in this situation?

Both feel love towards each other. There is warmth in their tone. But imagine if the woman reciprocates by saying, 'I **like** you too, my dear.' The man will be in an awkward and strange situation. Their emotional wavelengths do not match.

So in order to build a quick rapport, we need to match our words and tonality. Let's study a few scenarios.

Client: We are looking for a marketing automation platform.

The response of Seller 1: All right. We can give you a demo of our growth marketing platform and walk you through the success stories of our clients. When can we set up the meeting?

The response of Seller 2: All right. We can demo our marketing automation platform and also walk you through the success stories of our clients. When can we set up the meeting?

Client: I need to build a business case.

The response of Seller 1: Sure, we can help you with ROI calculations.

The response of Seller 2: Sure, we can work with you on creating a business case and include ROI calculations.

Did you notice the difference? Just adding a few similar words in the second response brings in the element of developing a connection with the client, which the first response fails to achieve.

Just like the similarity in the words, a similarity in the tone works as well. Do you feel good if the person you're speaking to is loud while you are talking in a nice, balanced tone? Or if they are speaking way too fast and you cannot understand half of what they are saying? A mismatch in tonality immediately hampers the rapport.

So the coordination of words, pitch, tone and speed of words can create an amazing environment. The same thing can be achieved in a telephone conversation.

Authentic, Well-Intentioned Praise

I love the saying, 'What you appreciate, appreciates.' To me, true praise is all about genuine appreciation.

I will always remember the handwritten notes of Ray Townsend (one of my managers) that said, 'Thanks Amit for your work over the weekend so that this important project could go live. Really appreciate your diligence. Here are two movie tickets for Ayesha and you. Take a break and have a good time.'

Believe it or not, this little incident happened seventeen years ago yet I still remember it and I always will. That is the power of authentic praise and appreciation.

Consider these praises:

'You look so handsome today in that suit.'

'Your responses in the client meeting were amazing. I really appreciate the way you stood by our team. Thank you.'

'Your blog is amazing. I have never seen someone sharing personal pains for the benefit of others. I learnt a lot from your story of coming out of debt.'

Imagine yourself to be at the receiving end of such praise. Won't you feel uplifted, happy and confident? Wouldn't it bring a smile to your face? Of course, it will! Praise has a high-energy vibration. It makes you feel positive and builds a strong connection with the person who has appreciated your work.

So how can you use praise to your advantage?

You can always do some research on social media before you meet someone for the first time and look out for personal or professional achievements. Congratulate them to start off on a friendly note.

'I noticed that your company has achieved a record 28 per cent net margin this quarter. Hearty congratulations to your team and you.'

'I read that your bank has won five awards in the customer experience category. That is a great achievement for your team and you.'

'I came across an article where you highlighted that the real pain of marketers is being able to connect all data sources and channels to the same hub. It was very well written and put together.'

Even in our personal lives, genuine appreciation is a great motivator for kids. My son Tanish beams with happiness when he is told, 'Tanish, for a twelve-year-old boy, you bowl so very fast. It is really amazing. When you were young, I used to bat left-handed. Now with your bowling speed, I have to resort to my normal right-hand stance.'

Often, praise is accompanied by a follow-up. What happens then? Look at these examples:

'You have done well in the last semester. Now work hard for the next semester.'

'Thanks to all your efforts, the last quarter was amazing. Now let's work hard during the next quarter too.'

As you can see, the follow-up negates the praise, even though it may be unintentional. The genuineness of the appreciation is substantially decreased and certain negativity creeps into the statement. Thus, it is simply not praise but **genuine** praise that is the key to developing a connection and rapport.

Mention Three Truths for Instant Rapport Building

We have all experienced multiple meetings throughout the week or sometimes even in a single day! Let's say you are about to begin one such meeting with a client. How would you start?

Option 1: You will exchange general pleasantries and start the presentation.

Option 2: You mention **three things** at the start of the meeting that are true to the client's situation or context.

For example: 'Thanks for finding time on a busy **Monday** morning to discuss your **advanced analytics** needs. It is nice to see that we have a representation of **all key** functions. We look forward to a very productive session.'

Notice the words in bold? They are **'Monday'**, **'advanced analytics'** and **'all key functions'**. These are the three items that would put clients at ease, create an atmosphere that is both comfortable and means business, and would make them say yes to you in their minds. Multiple such 'Yeses' when stacked together create a liking and build a rapport. Even after the initial rapport is built, using this technique in the interaction from time to time will help to maintain and build further rapport.

2. Two Magical Words

In Use Case Selling, I've noticed that certain words or phrases really work like magic when it comes to expressing your point of view in a way that is immediately understood by the clients. One such group of magical words is **It's Like**.

This phrase can be connected to the section on metaphors discussed in Chapter 2. There, we discussed how metaphors were a great tool for effective persuasion because they make communication simple by providing a reference point. And an easy way to create a metaphor is to use 'It's like' or 'Is like' as part of a three-step process.

The three-step process is as follows:

Step One: Take a situation.

Step Two: Think of what you would like to compare your situation/product/idea to.

Step Three: Use 'It's like' to connect 1 and 2.

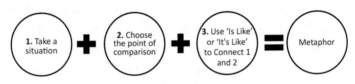

Fig. 9.1

Now let us create a metaphor.

Step 1: Take a situation.

It is both difficult and rewarding to win clients in start-ups when compared to large companies.

Step 2: Figure out the comparison.

Scoring centuries on bouncy and swinging pitches in England.

Step 3: Now we use 'It's like' and the metaphor is ready.

Winning clients in a start-up is very difficult, tests your skills and yet is very rewarding.

It's like scoring centuries on bouncy and swinging pitches in England. Both require deep focus, teamwork, a strong desire to succeed and, most importantly, Virat Kohli.

Now, you may wonder why the sudden inclusion of Virat Kohli. This was included to highlight the importance of relevant comparison. When you are thinking of a metaphor, always keep in mind the cultural background of the person or organization you are communicating with. For example, if you make a reference to Virat Kohli among clients who come from countries where cricket is not a popular sport, it just falls flat. So using genuine and relevant comparisons is the key to a successful metaphor.

Let's create another metaphor.

Situation: The CRM adoption is very low (10 per cent) for a particular client (Pinnacle Industries).

Point of Comparison: A family car having seven seats.

Final metaphor using 'It's like':

There are so many CRM capabilities that are valuable but lie unutilized at Pinnacle Industries. It's like having a high-end model of a seven-seater Toyota Innova Crysta and using it only for your office commute.

Metaphors

Become a persuasion powerhouse using two words

Scan the QR code to watch the video

Video: 2 mins   Video: 7 mins

3. The Magic of One Thing

As I had mentioned in the very first chapter, the book titled *The One Thing* has created a significant impact in many areas of my life. I have used this simple framework in my professional life and it has worked beautifully. By tweaking the One Thing question, I have made it suit my sales requirements:

What is the one thing I can do <area> <by time period> such that by doing it everything else would be easier or unnecessary?

Here are some examples of how asking the One Thing question can help in various sales scenarios:

Client Engagement

What is the one thing I can achieve in this client meeting such that . . .

What is the one slide we need to spend maximum time on for this client such that . . .

What is the one client need that we need to address to win this client such that . . .

What is the one point of differentiation I can highlight for my client such that . . .

What is the one client success story that we need to share to win this client such that . . .

Sales Planning

What is the one thing I can achieve in sales in this quarter such that it will de-risk the entire year . . .
What is the one support item I can get from <department name> such that it will enable me to exceed the sales target . . .

Team and Process

What is the one capability my sales team can develop such that . . .

What is the one change in the sales process I can invest in, in the first three months such that . . .

I hope the above examples have highlighted how easily the One Thing can be used in sales situations.

How the One Thing Is Used to Choose an Unconventional Growth Driver in a Start-up

Let me share a success story where asking this wonderful question helped me create a growth strategy for a start-up. This success story is contextualized against the backdrop of a time when we were discussing many different kinds of elements to fuel our sales growth over a period of the next one to three years. Some of the options under consideration were as follows:

- Changes in organizational structure
- Hiring more sales owners
- Creating newer product capabilities
- Opening in the US and more markets in Africa
- Relocating many sales owners to other regions
- Creating a pricing structure that could address our growth ambition

We could have gone ahead with any of these strategies as all of them are quite important. Yet, I felt that something was amiss. I wasn't feeling complete or satisfied with the choices at hand. Then, I asked myself the question:

What is the one thing we can do within the next three to six months that will fuel predictable growth for the next one to three years?

The answer I got took many of my colleagues by surprise. The answer was to focus on 100 per cent retention of existing accounts.

This may appear counterintuitive as our objective was fresh growth in sales. However, the rationale behind this was, 'Who would want to work with a start-up that can't even handle their existing clients?' The entire new sales strategy for this start-up was dependent on customers who would act as references and authenticate our work. And for customers to become references, they had to be retained. Interestingly, we executed this and it worked wonders in retaining our customers, which in turn fuelled the growth of new sales.

A Testimonial on the Magic of the One Thing in Sales: From Ashwin Khasnis

(https://www.linkedin.com/in/ashwin-khasnis-599aab17/)

I first met Ashwin at a hotel in Mumbai to interview him for a sales position. During the meeting, I shared the magic of One Thing with him. Within a few weeks, he WhatsApped me to thank me as he had cracked a large deal by using the magic of One Thing.

Here is Ashwin's account of what happened . . .

I first heard this concept of the One Thing from Amit when he was interviewing me for a sales position. I still remember that interview because it was so unconventional. Amit and I bonded over salesmanship and strategies. We discussed soft skills and our personal mantras in great detail.

Amit said, 'What is that one criterion which outweighs all the others and is the ultimate reason for the scales to tip in your favour? So, for a job change, is it the commute to work or a learning atmosphere or more salary or more freedom?'

We had to choose just one of the options. He went on to explain how the same strategy could be used for sales. Amit told me that in life, people always take decisions based on that one thing.

A few months later I tried to experiment with this concept of the One Thing in a sales call. I was interacting with several decision-makers and stakeholders during the deal. So we had the IT head, the head of marketing, the legal head and the end user of the product all present as active participants in the discussion.

At the end of the meeting, I asked them what would be the one thing that would make a difference to their decision. I got a different answer from every person present on that sales call.

IT head: Security protocols

Marketing head: ROI

Legal head: Compliance

End user: Customer support

Decision-maker: A business partner

After studying their individual requirements, I said, 'We will ensure that we meet all security protocols and compliance standards while giving you the best customer support and a satisfactory return on investment. I will ensure that we are just not a service provider but a trustworthy business partner for your company.'

What did I do here? I comforted each one of them personally by looking at each stakeholder's expectation from the deal. And it was the one thing question that had revealed the same.

A few days later, we won the account. We weren't the cheapest option for the client. However, it was our service-minded approach that addressed the one thing of concern for each decision-maker and that helped us greatly.

The magic of one thing in sales

How to achieve more in sales by doing less

Scan the QR code to watch the video

Summary View: How Three Tools and Five Mindsets Align with Use Case Selling

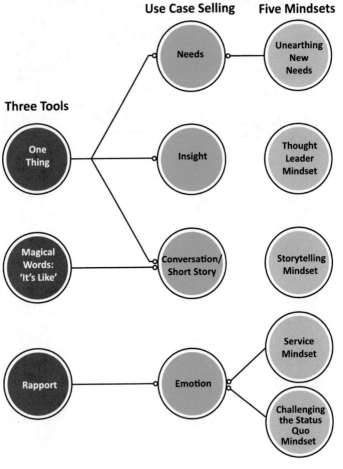

Fig. 9.2

Learning Accelerator

1. With the technique explained in the chapter, create a metaphor using 'It's like'.

    Think about a situation_____
    Choose a point of comparison_____
    Link the two with 'It's like'._____

2. Now that you have understood the magic of the One Thing, what is the one scenario in your professional or personal life where you can use the One Thing to move forward?

3. Among the techniques mentioned in the section on rapport, if you had to choose only one, which would you choose to implement from now on?

    ☐   Show me that you know me
    ☐   Physical mirroring and mapping
    ☐   Matching tonality and words
    ☐   Authentic, well-intentioned praise
    ☐   Three truths for instant rapport building

Chapter 10

How Does Use Case Selling Accelerate Virtual Selling?

The pandemic (COVID-19) changed the world in many ways.

✓ It helped us realize the importance of *anicca*, a Pali word that means impermanence. Lives, wealth and livelihoods were lost.
  - Seeing so many people die was very painful.
  - The stock market crashed.
  - Many people lost their jobs.

✓ It challenged our comfort zone by removing in-person socialization, and making social distancing and wearing masks mandatory.

✓ It changed the way the world did business. Remote work suddenly became the need of the hour. From non-acceptance, remote work became the norm in two years.

As discussed in chapter 1, an epic sale is similar to a David and Goliath story, where David emerges victorious . . . a victory that seemed improbable, yet created a milestone. The pandemic offered an opportunity to create epic sales for sales owners around the world.

Did the pandemic change the way companies sell and buyers buy?

The pandemic expedited the adoption of virtual selling globally. Virtual selling entailed completing all stages of a sale (qualification, client meetings, demos, workshops, negotiation, legal discussion, etc.) without meeting the customer.

The Benefits of Virtual Selling

✓ It decreases the cost of sales due to savings in travel costs.

✓ It increases market reach. It provides an opportunity to sell from anywhere rather than being in a specific region.

✓ It decreases the difference between big companies and early-stage start-ups.

Two key data points in the October 2020 McKinsey report[1] highlight that buyers and sellers embraced virtual selling.

1. Buyers and sellers handled ~70–80 per cent of the B2B buying process remotely or via digital self-service.

Current way of interacting with suppliers' sales reps during different stages[1,3]
% of respondents

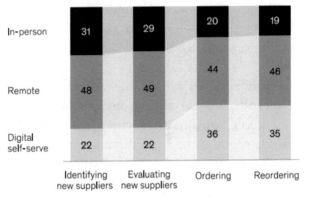

	Identifying new suppliers	Evaluating new suppliers	Ordering	Reordering
In-person	31	29	20	19
Remote	48	49	44	46
Digital self-serve	22	22	36	35

Fig. 10.1

2. B2B buyers were comfortable buying large-order-value items virtually.

Maximum order value you would purchase through end-to-end digital self-service and remote human interactions for a new product or service category[1,2]
% of respondents

Over $1M
amount **15%** are willing to spend

$500K to $1M
amount **12%** are willing to spend

$50K to $500K
amount **32%** are willing to spend

Fig. 10.2

While buyers embraced virtual selling, sales functions embraced virtual selling by focusing on three areas: **People, Processes and Tools**. Let's understand them . . .

People

In April 2020, I asked one of my team members '*Aap kaise ho*? (How are you?)'

He said, 'I don't have a job.'

Extremely surprised, I asked, 'You don't have a job?'

'Yes, I am sitting in a room for the entire day. I can't meet my customers. Thus, I don't have a job,' he said with a rueful smile.

That moment made me realize the pandemic's emotional impact on sales owners. Empathy and patience towards sales owners became easier after this experience.

Another sales owner in my team had a monk-like demeanour. Before the pandemic, he was always calm, composed and resourceful. Socializing with friends and meeting clients in person was very natural for him. The pandemic stopped both. I remember a calm and balanced sales owner snapping many times. While I was surprised by the sudden transition, my deep personal work in mindfulness since 2018 helped me harness the required empathy and patience.

This period highlighted the need for mindfulness in sales. Mindfulness practices such as meditation, gratitude, yoga, etc., help sales owners experience holistic wellness and strengthen emotional intelligence (EQ).

One of the things that helped my team and me during this period is the **3 S principle** in sales. The 3 S principle says:

'To make selling a fulfilling experience, we need to harness *Shradha* (faith), *Saburi* (patience) and *Sadhana* (disciplined action).'

THREE 'S' REQUIRED FOR SALES

Fig. 10.3

Shradha (faith): In the scriptures, it is written, 'Faith can move mountains.'

Imagine what can happen, when you experience:

Faith in your company,
Faith in your product, service or idea,
Faith in your clients,
Faith in your team,
Faith in the universe,
and most important, Faith in yourself.

Saburi (patience): Patience has always been a virtue. Which of these three quotes on patience resonates the most with you?

'One minute of patience, ten years of peace'
—Greek proverb

'Patience attracts happiness; it brings near that which is far'
—Swahili proverb

'To lose patience is to lose the battle'

—Mahatma Gandhi

During the pandemic, the changing sales scenarios and the need for mental wellness reminded us to be more patient than ever.

Sadhana (disciplined action): Disciplined action requires identifying and executing priority activities among the many that help deal movement. To implement this, we created a 'Path to Contract Signature (PTCS)'.

PTCS contained a list of action items required until the contract signature.

S. No.	Action Category	Action Items Description	Owner	Date	Priority Task	Comments

For priority tasks, we identified up to three[2] tasks. Among them, we always ask and remind ourselves of the single most important task. We were implementing the One Thing principle.

Processes

A major change in sales during the pandemic was engaging customers and closing the deal without meeting

[2] Many applications of the Rule of Three are given in the productivity section of my book *Small is Big*.

in person. This led to the popularization of the term 'virtual selling'. The virtual selling process requires four key adoption levers:

Fig. 10.4

✓ *Embrace virtual meeting platforms*
   Sales owners used virtual meeting platforms like Zoom, Microsoft Team and Webex even before the pandemic. During the pandemic, it became the **only** option for client engagement as in-person engagement was impossible. I observed that high-performance sellers treated virtual space with the same rigor as meeting a client in person. Here are three examples:

- They dressed in business attire during virtual meetings.
- They had the right team representation. Joining virtually actually made it easier to involve anyone as travel was not needed.
- They prepared well in advance to create maximum impact in a thirty-to-sixty-minute virtual meeting.

✓ *Switch video on*
   Renowned behavioural psychologist Dr Albert Mehrabian postulated the 7-38-55[3] rule to highlight the impact of verbal and non-verbal communication.

As per the rule, 7 per cent of meaning is communicated through the spoken word, 38 per cent through the tone of voice, and 55 per cent through body language.

Type of Communication and associated impact

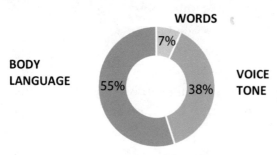

Fig. 10.5

Video engagement is needed in virtual selling to help sales owners harness non-verbal aspects of communication such as facial expressions, gestures, posture and other body movements. Non-verbal communication is essential because it creates rapport and emotional bonding.[4]

In a way, video engagement was the next best alternative to in-person meetings.

Three Simple Tips for Improving Video Experience during Virtual Meetings

1. Right video frame: Head and shoulders of the speaker need to be visible. The gap between the head and the top of the screen can be around one inch.

2. Light source: To ensure that your face and shoulders are lit well, use sunlight or an external light source.
3. Video on duration: If switching the video on for the entire meeting duration is tiring, switch the video on while starting and ending the client meeting. During the meeting, you can switch the video on when you are speaking.

✓ *Creating a compelling narrative*
    To create a compelling narrative in virtual selling, we use principles from Use Case Selling.

The One Thing Principle

The One Thing principle helped my team and me in creating a compelling narrative. We asked the following question: *If we have to share only one message or slide that would create maximum value for the client, which one would we share?*

This question made us responsible and helped us prepare well in advance. Let me share an example.

While presenting to the chief digital officer (CDO) of one large retailer in Asia, we compared the customer experience on the retailer's website with the customer experience of three other competitors. The narrative was insightful, provocative and created a contrast. It was only one slide.

Metaphors

Metaphors work in virtual selling because they create visual stories instantaneously.

Among many metaphors, here's one of the metaphors we have used with a client.

A customer data platform is like a human brain; marketing automation is like the hands and legs. You have a choice:

1. *Having a brain from someone and hands and legs from others.*
2. *Having a brain, hands and legs from one vendor.*

The client ended up choosing **all** marketing solutions from my company.

Insightful Content

During the pandemic, clients were swamped with vendors asking for their attention. They also experienced digital fatigue. While always needed, contextual and insightful communication became the need of the hour.

I remember one large retailer in Asia sharing five specific use cases for personalizing the digital experience. We responded:

'Thanks for sharing five use cases. We would be happy to show a live demo for the same. We are sharing five additional use cases that progressive retailers like yourself should implement to personalize digital experiences. Please review. We would demonstrate these use cases also in our discussion.'

The example shared with the CDO using the One Thing principle above was also insightful because it presented competitive benchmarking on customer experience, which customers didn't know about.

Want to Be Charismatic and Trustworthy? Just Use Your Hands

You have created a compelling narrative and now you have to deliver it. Can making hand movements help you? Science of People, a human behaviour consultancy firm, researched[5] on why a few TED Talks go viral.

They used 760 volunteers to rate TED Talks posted on TED.com in 2010, which were between fifteen and twenty minutes long.

What they found out was fascinating:

The bottom TED Talks had an average of 1,24,000 views and used an average of 272 hand gestures during the eighteen-minute talk. The top TED Talks had an average of 7,360,000 views and used an average of 465 hand gestures—that's almost double!

Temple Grandin[6] (6.4m views), Jane McGonigal[7] (6.2m views), Simon Sinek[8] (59m views) topped the hand movement charts with over 600 hand gestures.

The more hand gestures, the more successful the TED Talk.

This happened because non-verbal hand movements made the speaker more credible, charismatic and trustworthy.

In virtual selling, using one's hands while speaking could be a game changer because only the upper portion of the body is visible.

   ✓ *Sharing personalized videos with clients*

Short videos on product capability, business use cases, success stories and proposal summaries are great for virtual client engagement. Besides formal videos, we also used WhatsApp to share informal videos with prospects. To cultivate video creation, we included them as part of quarterly objectives and key results (OKR).

We started small with four videos per quarter per sales owner and then moved to twelve videos per quarter per sales owner. Over time, video creation became more straightforward, and we could create a video repository.

Tools

Tools played a crucial role in virtual selling adoption. Among the plethora of tools, I am sharing the ones that matter most.

- Virtual meeting platforms: Zoom, Microsoft Teams, Webex, Google Meet, GoToMeeting
- Video recording: Loom, Vidyard
- Social selling: LinkedIn, LinkedIn Sales Navigator
- Document tracking: LinkedIn Smart links, HubSpot
- Editing: Grammarly
- Presentation: Microsoft PowerPoint, Keynote

A Virtual Presentation Tip: Using Annotations and Animations to engage your audience and help them retain information

Annotations help you bring your audience's attention to a specific area and create **contrast**. This can be done in the following ways:
- Use dotted rectangles or any other shape to highlight a section of the slide.

- Draw (or write) during the presentation using annotation capabilities in PowerPoint[9] or a video platform (like Zoom). The mouse pointer or a touchscreen pencil can be used for the same.

Animations[10] in PowerPoint help us to pace our content better. Instead of introducing the entire slide, one can create animations to improve the speed and timing of introducing the content in our presentation. This helps the viewers easily process the information and retain it better.

CAPITALIZE ON CONTRAST

Six examples of how to engage audience virtually

Scan the QR code to watch the video

Having understood the people, process and technology aspects of virtual selling, let's look at the virtual selling success story during the pandemic using the four pillars of Use Case Selling.

When a Loss-Making Client Bought an Entire Growth Marketing Product Stack during the Pandemic

We worked on a marquee quick service restaurant (QSR) prospect for four months and had deep interactions with the CIO, CMO, COO, head of analytics and other leaders. QSR brands are names like Domino's, Pizza Hut, KFC, McDonald's and Burger King. I was deeply involved in this deal because the brand had a global presence. Engagement in one country can fuel engagements in multiple countries. We had reached a stage where one final discussion was required with the client COO, the economic buyer.

With a lot of excitement about the deal and a bit of fear due to the pandemic, I flew to Mumbai on 6 January 2020 to meet the COO and finalize contractual formalities.

I remember the date distinctly because it was my first flight with a mask and the last flight before the lockdown. I took a flight again after almost one and a half years.

First flight with a mask

The meeting went very well, and the COO asked the CIO to proceed with the contract.

In March, the lockdown started due to the pandemic. The dream of getting a multicountry account was becoming hazy. Initially, my sales team and I kept in touch with the CIO, and he kept saying that we were progressing. After one month, progress stopped because the pandemic severely impacted this company in the form of store closures, revenue loss and declining stock price. Considering the sensitive situation, we exercised empathy and patience and gave the situation time to improve.

The pandemic situation didn't improve. In August 2020, one sales team member reached out to the client COO on LinkedIn, and the COO replied that we should talk again. It was a welcome sign.

During the initial conversations, we came to know that the CIO was leaving and that the client had signed another vendor for a marketing automation tool.

For a moment, I was both surprised and hurt. Surprised by both developments and hurt by the second one.

The CIO leaving was a big setback. We had to find a new champion.

The marketing automation vendor selection hurt because I was asking the following questions:

Why did they sign with an alternative when they had initiated a contract with us?

Why did they not reach out to us while evaluating the other alternative?

I reached out one-on-one to the CMO and the COO separately and expressed my pain, surprise and displeasure.

The CMO said, 'Amit ji, this is an alternative for a few months because we wanted a cheaper solution for a minimal scope. Also, the vendor introduction came from the board. This is not for our larger analytics vision, which we have scoped with your company.'

The COO said, 'Arré Amit, this solution is for just Rs 1 lakh per month, and I can terminate it any time. Just a stop-gap arrangement till we initiate the larger project with you. The alternative solution is sending communication, which lacks intelligence. It's like a dumb box. Intelligence will come from your analytics solution.'

Relieved by their response, I asked the COO, 'Why do you want to pursue the project now during such difficult times?'

The client answered, 'We are in August 2020. We want to be ready when store opening picks up momentum in January 2021.'

Since they had marketing automation from another vendor, they decided to go ahead with my company's customer data platform (CDP). In a subsequent discussion, the COO and CMO said, 'Your company would be responsible for business impact.'

I asked why.

The COO said, 'This is because intelligence lies in your CDP platform.'

I said, 'Yes, CDP is like the brain in the body and marketing automation is like the hands and legs. Since you have two vendors, it's like two different bodies. Thus, assigning business impact responsibility to one vendor would be difficult.'

The COO was quiet for a while and then said, 'Let me reflect . . .'

A few days later, the client team came back and said that they needed marketing automation also from my company.

Due to our recent merger with another company, we had a new product, a customer experience platform (CXP), which personalized online experiences on websites and apps. In simple terms, it gave an experience that was **better** than the buying experience on Amazon.

The pandemic enabled customers to adopt online channels. I reached out to the COO and said, 'The pandemic offers an opportunity to invest in curating online experiences to drive sales. Personalizing online experiences on the website or app in the QSR industry is in the very early stage of adoption. Business opportunity and low adoption present a great opportunity for your brand to be the first in the region to provide these experiences to your customer. What do you think?'

Within seconds, he said, 'This makes sense. Please arrange a demo of CXP.'

Apart from the demo, we also compared the online customer experience with two other competitors.

This resulted in the client agreeing to buy CXP also.

I remember distinctly that the contract was signed during Diwali in 2020. This created a lot of joy and hope within the sales team and the entire company during difficult times.

So from the contract being halted, the CIO leaving and a new vendor on the account, we ended up signing three product lines with a global QSR brand during the pandemic. It was an Epic Sale. From 6 March 2020 to October 2020, we didn't meet even a single time in person during those nine months. Our Sales team engaged the client virtually using Use Case Selling, the 3 S principle: Shradha, Saburi and Sadhana, and the virtual selling process and tools mentioned above.

Let's analyse this epic sale using the four-pillar Use Case Selling Model.

Need: CDP and marketing automation were known and unmet needs of the client. CXP was an unknown need and was not even part of the scope. Having one partner for all product lines was an unmet need with resistance to change.

Insight: Introducing CXP for personalizing the experience on the website and app was new for the client and the entire QSR segment in Asia. We also showed the customer experience comparison with other QSR brands and client competitors.

Using the metaphor of brain, hands and legs provided an insight that made them realize the difficulty in making one vendor responsible for business impact amidst multiple vendors.

Conversation or Short Story: Among various conversations, asking questions and using a metaphor had the maximum impact.

Questions: The following questions triggered empathy and conversation from the client:

Why did you not select us for marketing automation?

Why did you not call us while evaluating alternatives?

Metaphor: The metaphor works because it creates *visual stories* instantaneously. The client was okay with having multiple vendors even though business impact responsibility was given to one vendor.

In this case, the metaphor of the brain, hands and legs helped me convey the point that the client had not considered. A simple metaphor achieved what multiple logical discussions would have failed to.

Emotion: This deal triggered two sets of emotions.

My emotions (Anxiety): Human beings are kind at heart and care for other humans. Emotions, when shared authentically, create empathy. When I shared my pain and displeasure about selecting another vendor, the client CMO and the COO understood my pain and provided empathetic explanations. Some of their responses, as given above, show the emotional charge triggered in them due to my pain.

The client COO emotions: Being the first in the region to adopt CXP created an emotion of aspiration within the COO.

Not being able to measure business impact clearly due to two vendors created anxiety.

Being the first brand to integrate CDP, marketing automation and CXP created a growth vision for the future for the client.

As in the above example, an epic sale was possible due to the adoption of Use Case Selling in a virtual context. The four NICE pillars of Use Case Selling are holistic and cover any situation in business and in life.

Virtual Selling Checklist

S. No.	Virtual Selling Implementation Lever	Adoption
1	**People**	
1.1	3 S Principle (Shradha, Saburi, Sadhana)	☐
1.2	Mindfulness practice	
	Meditation	☐
	Gratitude	☐
	Sports	☐
	Exercise (yoga, running, gym, etc.)	☐
	Others	☐
1.3	Having a pleasant smile	☐
2	**Process**	
2.1	Switch video on during virtual client meetings	☐
2.2	Use the right frame with face and shoulders visible. The gap between the head and the top of the screen is around one inch	☐
2.3	Use hands while speaking	☐
2.4	Create a minimum of one video per week	☐
2.5	Adopt the Use Case Selling four pillars checklist	☐

3	Tools	
3.1	Virtual meeting platforms	☐
3.2	HD webcam	☐
3.3	Quality headphones	☐
3.4	Additional light source (if required)	☐
3.5	Video creation tools (e.g., Vidyard, Loom, etc.)	☐
3.6	Content editing tools (Grammarly)	☐
3.7	Social selling tools	
	LinkedIn	☐
	LinkedIn Sales Navigator	☐
	Others	☐
3.8	Annotations and Animations	☐

Learning Accelerator

1. What is the 3 S principle for holistic sales?
    a) S_____
    b) S_____
    c) S_____

2. Which part is most difficult for you in virtual selling?
    a) Meeting clients remotely rather than
        in person   ☐
    b) Creating compelling narratives   ☐
    c) Continuous video engagement   ☐
    d) Using new-age virtual selling tools   ☐

3. For your responses in question 2, please identify up
    to three action items to address the difficulty.
    a) _____
        _____
    b) _____
        _____
    c) _____
        _____

Chapter 11

Who Is the Sales Owner of the Future?

'The best way to predict your future is to create it'
—Abraham Lincoln

For quite some time, in 2013, I used to be overcome by extreme fatigue at the end of every day. So in November 2013, I decided to consult an Ayurvedic physician in Bangalore to try and cure this strange tiredness that was taking a severe toll on me. After checking my pulse, the doctor looked concerned. She clicked her tongue several times to express her displeasure. Naturally, it got me worried and I waited anxiously for her to say something.

'Do you have a history of diabetes in your family?' she asked. Her question surprised me. Here I was seeking a remedy for my general fatigue and she was asking me about diabetes.

'Yes, my parents are diabetic.'

'All right, your pulse indicates that you are pre-diabetic. Please do a few tests and meet me after three days. You must do them because it is only then that I can confirm.'

The doctor's initial diagnosis had me stressed. I thought I was too young to be pre-diabetic. I was mentally unprepared but went ahead with the tests. When I returned to her clinic, my reports validated her diagnosis. I was a clear borderline case of diabetes.

She recommended a few medicines but most importantly, asked me to completely stop consuming all forms of sugar. This was very difficult for me because I had quite a sweet tooth. I asked if I could eat my favourite gajar ka halwa (carrot pudding) for a few days during the winter and if I could continue with sugar in my tea. She said a strict NO to both. I was taken aback.

For one and a half years, I distanced myself from all forms of sugar. It was very tough for me to refuse when my two sons offered their birthday cakes. But I knew that my health was at stake. If I gave in to temptation, the end result would be terrible. Now I am out of my pre-diabetic condition and my cravings for sugar are gone. For both, I am very grateful to the excellent doctor who identified this condition proactively and gave me strict instructions about disciplining my lifestyle.

Why is this story relevant to my book on Use Case Selling?

This is because I firmly believe that the profile of a successful future sales owner is very similar to that of a specialist doctor.

A specialist doctor denotes excellence in two areas: *expertise* and *communication*.

- Excellence in expertise creates trust and certainty.

- Excellence in communication creates rapport and warmth.

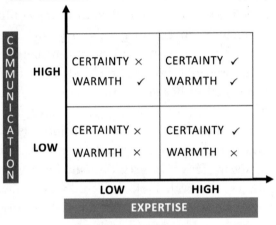

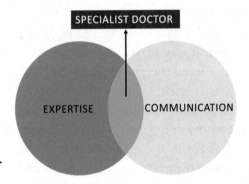

Fig. 11.1

Just as doctors have their areas of specialization, a sales owner will be a thorough expert and a thought leader in his or her field.

As a doctor delves into the medical state of a patient and finds the problem, a sales owner studies the situation and will be able to unearth the unknown needs and problems of the customers.

As a doctor connects with the patient, a sales owner will build a rapport with their clients.

As a doctor suggests remedies, a sales owner will prescribe solutions and put forward corrective action that would remedy the customer's situation.

A specialist doctor is a *symbol* of sales excellence for everyone who is selling a product, service or idea, e.g. organizations, sales teams, marketing teams, CEOs, websites, sales owners, etc.

Which symbol represents a sales owner in a complex sales environment?

Scan the QR code to watch the video

Through the Use Case Selling strategy, I wish to provide a very simple and extremely effective framework for sales owners to emerge as excellent doctors who successfully understand the needs of their clients and service them to the best of their capabilities. I trust it will create epic sales for you in business and in life!

ALL THE BEST!

Epilogue

Who Will Harness the True Spirit of Sales?

What does sales represent in its true spirit?

I kept asking myself these questions primarily because of the negative connotation the word 'sales' brings to mind.

Interestingly, I got the answer to this question during my morning meditation. The word SALES represents the following:

S—Serve *with*
A—Authenticity
L—Love
E—Expertise *and*
S—Smile

As I opened my eyes after meditating, I smiled and thanked the universe for giving me such a profound answer.

Now, who can undertake such SALES? Is it a sales owner or a Salespreneur?

A Salespreneur believes that sales is social entrepreneurship because every sale is an opportunity to bring in **Joy**, generate a **Livelihood,** create **Value** for customers and build **Wealth** for the economy.

SALESPRENEUR
Creating an Ecosystem for Epic Sales

Bringing in Joy

What happens when a sales owner receives and shares a purchase order with his team and other stakeholders?

A sense of fulfilment and happiness and joy takes over. People smile and congratulate each other. In many organizations, I have seen celebrations after client wins. This creates a festive environment.

Generating a Livelihood

In 2012, something happened that changed my perspective on the importance of sales.

I was sitting in a conference room with my team for a sales review when I asked them something unusual.

'Do you recognize the importance and impact of your work?' Of course, this question was surprising as people were expecting a traditional sales review.

I waited for an answer for a few seconds and then said in Hindi, '*Aapke kaam ke karan ek sau assi logon ke ghar mein roti banti hai* (Due to your work, bread is getting cooked in 180 households)!'

180 was the number of employees in the start-up.

I'm not sure what prompted me to say these lines but even while they were leaving my mouth, I could sense that I was having a hair-raising experience. As my team members heard this, I could see a sense of pride and emotion transforming everyone's faces.

Something shifted within me on that day and that scene has remained with me. It reminds me of the impact of sales beyond traditional numbers. This brings in an extreme sense of responsibility and fulfilment.

Creating Value for Customers

A Salespreneur is inspired by the mission to create value for his/her customers and make them shine.

A Salespreneur identifies value criteria upfront for his/her customers and works with the customer to track them regularly.

Driving Economic Growth

Economic growth is the sum of all profitable sales in a country. If sales decrease, economic growth decreases, and recession follows.

Imagine a day when no sale happens in the world. What will happen to stock markets?

The notion that 'Sales drive economic growth at the country level' is profound and brings out the required ownership.

As discussed in this book, all of us are in sales because we are all selling products, services or ideas. Imagine what the world would be if all of the 7.7 billion sales owners become Salespreneurs and harness the true spirit of the word SALES.

What does the word 'sales' really mean?

Scan the QR code to watch the video

Who will harness the true spirit of sales?

Scan the QR code to watch the video

Bonus Material

Living *The Ultimate Sales Accelerator:* Readers' Success Stories

In a ten-day Vipassana meditation course, I learnt that there are three kinds of wisdom:

Received wisdom: Wisdom acquired by reading or listening to others, e.g., reading this book

Intellectual wisdom: Wisdom acquired by examining received wisdom rationally and logically, e.g., analysing the four parts of Use Case Selling and developing a point of view on why Use Case Selling is more effective than other forms of selling

Experiential wisdom: Wisdom acquired by implementation on oneself. This is the highest form of wisdom because it comes from the implementation of learnings. The implementation helps us harness our own wisdom based on our direct experience, e.g., implementing Use Case Selling in your business and/or life

This section covers the experiential wisdom of a few readers, who have implemented Use Case Selling. May these stories inspire you.

How My Wife and I Used Use Case Selling to Re-Enrol Our Six-Year-Old Daughter in Kung Fu Classes

Abhishek Kumar, sales director, Algonomy
https://www.linkedin.com/in/abhishek-kumar18/

The Ultimate Sales Accelerator is a wonderful book that outlines sales skills used in both professional and personal life. I was among the first ones to grab this book and have been adopting the learnings ever since.

One such use case (as the book refers to situations) I would like to share is from my personal life. I had enrolled my daughter in kung fu classes when she was six years old. While she was very excited in the beginning, her interest level started to drop gradually. Both my wife and I were trying all sorts of tricks, as I have mentioned below:

1. Motivating: Don't you want to get a black belt?
2. Comparison: Do you know one of the girls in our society has a black belt? We really want you to get that too.

3. Forcing: You must go, you don't have a choice.
4. Bribing: If you attend all classes this month, you get 'x'.
5. Many other tricks.

One day, both my wife and I decided to use the NICE framework (Need, Insight, Conversation, Emotion) and see if it really works in personal life. Therefore, we changed our conversation to the following:

'Riyansha (my daughter's name), you always say that you are grown up now, right? If yes, then why do you ask me to come along with you when you see strangers around you?'

She replied, 'Because you are stronger than me, Papa.'

I asked, 'Do you think that if you become a black belt, you would need my protection any more? If not, would this make you happier and more confident? In fact, I would want you to be around me and protect me.'

Of course, her answer was that she would be the strongest. Then I asked her to tell me five things she would want to do when she becomes stronger (black belt).

The entire conversation was on the NICE framework about her need, insight, conversation and emotion about aspiration. Since then, her interest level shot up and she started going regularly.

It may sound simple but it requires discipline to get this framework in daily life. Thanks to Amit for writing this book and inspiring a larger community.

How the book help me understand the deeper meaning of sales

Jaspreet Dhingra, founder, BANC, a B2B networking community
https://www.linkedin.com/in/jaspreet-dhingra-4104a36/

As we transition from the corporate world to starting our own business or start-up, one of the biggest challenges is to generate sales or revenues. Coming from a professional background and never having been in sales, I also faced a similar challenge while building BANC, a B2B networking community that is spread across seven countries now.

The one thing that *The Ultimate Sales Accelerator* helped me with was changing my perspective about looking at sales. The mantra is that when you are selling something, follow the approach of 'how is my product or service going to be helpful for that person', and how would it add value. Approach it with the purpose of serving the customer's needs and not sales. It has worked really well for me because when you are coming from this angle, your confidence, approach and pitch changes for good and the chances of success and building long-term relationships are much higher.

I continue to share this approach with my community members and have invited Amit also to share more insights from his book so that we can spread the word and make people fall in love with sales.

How I found the One Thing for my business

Avnish Sharma, founder and CEO, Syscraft Information System
https://www.linkedin.com/in/sharmaavnish/

I met Amit in a workshop organized by NASSCOM in Indore and he placed great emphasis on the power of the One Thing and how it can be utilized in sales. We continued our discussion post the session and I shared with him my experiences with the book *The Ultimate Sales Accelerator*. When Amit suggested using the concept of the One Thing in sales, initially I was a bit reluctant as we were so used to doing all the things we could to generate leads, from cold calling to networking to emailing to paid ads and whatnot.

At Syscraft, when I sat with my team to identify that One Thing that we can focus on to promote our sales and what USP we have to showcase, we ended up with a single word 'Reliability'. We started planning our sales around one word: *Reliability*. Some of the clients have been working with us for sixteen-plus years, and we got those who have been with us for more than ten years to share their experiences. We then prepared our case studies and started sharing those with our sales pitch. The one word, that one thing we brought on the table worked wonders not just to retain our other clients but to get new clients with ease.

In IT, with technology upgrading so fast and clients having dynamic requirements, we brought out the word of Long Relationships and Reliability. Our readiness to go the extra mile for our clients to keep them with us brought out a new perspective on sales.

That One Workshop, One Meeting, the One Book (*The Ultimate Sales Accelerator*) brought out the real sense of the One Thing for us in sales. All thanks to Amit, it made life easy for my sales team and for me.

How using ethos, pathos, logos helps me in pipeline development

**Santosh K.,
sales development
representative,
Indusface**
https://www.linkedin.com/in/
santosh-k-46407bb7/

I first came across the Greek philosopher Aristotle's key persuasion—ethos, logos, pathos—in the book *The Ultimate Sales Accelerator*.

Since then, I have been regularly using ethos, logos and pathos either in my sales pitches or emails as an effective way of communicating about the company and its product offerings. I work as an SDR (inbound sales with Indusface) who has to qualify the accounts/prospects for the next round of discussion.

You must be wondering how did I use ethos, logos, pathos in my sales pitches and emails? Here you go:

Ethos: It highlights the credibility of the brand
Indusface is purely an application security company; that's our forte. We have been in this space for more than fifteen years now.

We were a bootstrapped profitable organization and now we are a funded company. In fact, we got our funding in the midst of COVID-19 from Tata Capital Growth Fund. It has been a good run so far with 90 per cent YoY growth, and we have 3000+ global customers across thirty-six countries.

Pathos: Appeals to the emotions of the prospects
(Talking to an insurance company)
We have been working closely with BFSI companies since our inception. Would you be interested to learn how we helped XYZ insurance company with their legacy applications to virtually patch and protect their online assets? How are you placed this week?

These approaches have helped me become a trusted adviser and have super-engaged prospects, which eventually moved to pipeline.

How highlighting unmet needs improved email conversion rates

**Yash Agrawal,
founder,
Curious About Sales**
https://www.linkedin.com/in/
yashpagrawal/

I came across one of Amit Sir's posts on LinkedIn and decided to buy his book *The Ultimate Sales Accelerator*.

I have found tremendous value in using the Use Case Selling model in the cold emails we send to generate leads for our agency clients.

Let me explain.

Based on research, we find out what the unmet need of our prospect is.

Then in the cold emails, we share insights that the prospect does not know or what their competitors are doing to solve this problem/unmet need.

This immediately creates interest in the mind of the reader and we have seen our email response rates to be much better than when we tried to present benefits or features.

How Use Case Selling helped me ace an interview

Mamatha Shanmugam,
Technology Architect
https://www.linkedin.com/in/
mamatha-shanmugam/

I never thought a techie like me could ever wear a salesman's hat. When I first read Amit's book, I wondered why there wasn't a book like this earlier! This is what exactly I needed for my KPI 'Sell while Delivering'.

The use case technique, particularly the user vs buyer approach, is simple yet so powerful and impactful. Instead of focusing on the technical aspects I now focus on addressing the needs of the user, resulting in engaging conversations and creating the possibilities of new connections. Sales as a skill is not only required for B2B or B2C, it's required for everything we do. I realized this when I cracked a job interview for a cloud service provider, which is a market leader, and clearing their interview is very challenging. After spending eighteen-plus years with one IT giant, I decided to pursue other career opportunities. That's when I started thinking about how anyone could sell themselves in an interview. Yes! To me, this entire hiring process is a user (in this context the recruiter) buying the product (which is myself). As an experienced professional, I know I have so many things or features to my credit. However, how do I gain the trust and confidence of my recruiter in that forty-five to sixty-minute timeframe? Having read and understood the Use Case Selling technique, I decided to use it. For almost all my responses to users (recruiters), I used this technique and it worked (sold the product, which is me). So now I am a techie who can sell as well, both in business and on the personal front. Looking forward to your next book, Amit.

How I started crafting Unique Buying Propositions for my customers

**Nayan Kurup,
founder,
Cassini Technology
Consulting**
https://www.linkedin.com/in/
nayankurup/

Amit's spectacular book—*The Ultimate Sales Accelerator*—introduced the concept of Use Case Selling to me. The clarity with which he explained the four pillars—NICE (Need, Insight, Conversation/short stories, Emotion)—has helped tremendously, especially while pitching our products and services to potential clients. I have started approaching my presentations differently and ensuring I address the four aspects with utmost clarity.

We at Cassini Technology Consulting acquired a customer after implementing the strategy of Use Case Selling. I personally would also like to highlight the importance of understanding the five mindsets and the three tools while analysing and implementing the Use Case Selling strategy for the business.

The example below highlights how we have used two specific concepts given in the book: **'Show me that you know me'** and **'UPP—Unique Pain Point'**.

By using the technique of 'Show me that you know me' given in the book, we conducted our research on the potential client, which included reading about the industry the customer belonged to and understanding the pain points of the industry around the business process we were building the solution for. We used that information to build a proposal about industry best practices and the benefits the industry saw with regard to automation.

We requested the client to let us schedule a call with the key business user for a session to have a detailed understanding of the issues faced and the pain areas.

Aligning the technique 'Show me that you know me' to collect information on the expectations of the users, along with focusing on the service mindset, mainly on the concept of UPP of the client backed with industry research and best practices that we had zeroed down after analysing the research data, helped me structure my proposal.

While addressing their pain areas and how we at Cassini could support their functions and ensure smooth operations, I could say they valued our services and realized the importance of coming on board with us.

I closely witnessed how the UPP transformed into a Unique Buying Proposition and we successfully got the project. I would like to extend my sincere gratitude to Amit for his book, which has explained the concepts of sales with utmost ease. Your book has truly transformed my approach to sales and business.

How a nine-year-old helped me get a job

Tahseen Kazi,
Content Strategist
https://www.linkedin.com/in/
tahseen-kazi/

I use the concept of Use Case Selling regularly. But a section of the book that deeply resonated with me is the framework of Ethos–Logos–Pathos. In this section, Amit talks about an incident with his son, Aarav, who convinces his dad to do something that started with a clear 'no'. For me, this was the high point of the book. Here, Aarav beautifully uses logos and pathos to turn around an (almost) impossible request (sale) in his favour. It made me think that if a nine-year-old can be a great salesperson, so can anybody else.

One of the first places I distinctly remember trying out this persuasion framework was in a job interview. I led the process with ethos. One of the first questions I asked myself was, *What can I do to build credibility?* And I asked this question repeatedly till I found my solution. I created a customized video for the position and sent it along with my résumé. I also connected with the HR on LinkedIn and shared a personalized message with him while applying for the role. My first step towards building credibility was successful; I got a call for an interview.

While I started out strong in my first interview, I faltered midway by responding to a question with a mindless answer. I was determined not to give up though. I focused on the framework. At the end of the interview, I was asked how I would rate myself on a scale of one to ten. I was honest and said, 'If I were you, I wouldn't call me back for the next round.' By being honest and aware, I strengthened my credibility with this employer.

I used logos for the interview round in which I was required to complete an assignment. I made sure to cite data, facts, use cases and examples that supported my solution to the problem, emphasizing the logical approach I took in solving the problem.

In the final round, I used all three aspects of the framework, but pathos was what I relied on most. I brought my authentic self to the interview. I displayed the emotions of happiness, humour, vulnerability, empathy and disappointment in response to what was happening in a thoughtful manner. Using these emotions helped me connect better with the interviewer at a personal level rather than keeping the conversation transactional.

And then the rest, as they say, is history. I got the job. ☺

One Suggestion to Get the Most Out of This Book

Using the checklist given in chapter 4, implement the Use Case Selling principles in a minimum of **ten** sales scenarios in business or life within ninety days of reading this book. This will help expedite your learning process, deepen your knowledge and develop experiential wisdom. Wishing you godspeed. 🙏

The Four Pillars of Use Case Selling	Y/N	Comments
Need		
Addresses a specific, unserviced need (known need that is not met OR known need that resists change OR unknown need)		
Insights		
Shares valuable information that the customer doesn't know		
Shares valuable information about what other players in the market are doing, including client success stories, market research and analysis		
Conversation or Short Stories		
Uses questions and/or stories and/or metaphors and/or visuals to involve the user		
Does not involve any technical jargon		
Establishes a contrast to highlight the gap between the existing state and the desired state		
Emotion		
Triggers emotions of aspiration (gain) and/or anxiety (pain)		

The Sales Prayer

While writing the book, the universe helped me understand the deeper meaning of sales.

S—Serve *with*
A—Authenticity
L—Love
E—Expertise *and*
S—Smile

Considering the above, I use the following as a prayer:

May I serve with authenticity, love, expertise and smile 🙏

May my family serve with authenticity, love, expertise and smile 🙏

May all human beings serve with authenticity, love, expertise, and smile 🙏

Frequently Asked Questions (FAQs)

In this section, I have curated a set of ten questions that I am often asked in the context of Sales and Use Case Selling.

1. **When do insights not work?**

   Insights lead to action. If there is no action on the deal, this can be due to three scenarios:

   ✓ The buyer is not progressive

   Insights often address unknown needs. To address unknown needs, buyers must be progressive and change catalysts.

   ✓ Organizational structure dynamics

   In complex B2B sales, you are selling to a group of buyers who work in a matrix structure. If the deal is not moving, ask, *'Were we able to create insights for all buyers?'*

   ✓ Relevance to the organizational context

   For example, you delivered an insight on the growth of the online business. The prospect's total revenue is $100 million, and its online revenue is $1.5 million. The size of an online business is tiny for an insight to make an impact. Such experiences may help you refine your ideal customer profile (ICP).

2. **Which is the most challenging need to address within the Mount Everest of Needs?**
    An unmet need with resistance to change is the most challenging need because change is difficult.
    This happens because:

    - We are influenced by status quo bias: 'If it ain't broke, don't fix it'
    - As per loss aversion theory, our anxiety of loss is higher than the aspiration for gain

A few examples of unmet needs with resistance to change:
    - Life: Waking up at 5 a.m.
    - Business: Adoption of CRM by the sales team
    - Use Case Selling and the 3S Principle: Shradha–Saburi–Sadhana can help evangelize the why, what and how of change.

3. **How can I make closure a habit?**
    To make closure a habit, start looking at everything as sales deals and closing them. Sounds strange ☺. Let's look at a few examples.

    - *Paying the EMI or electricity bill or children's school fees on time*

- *Booking tickets for a family vacation*
- *Submitting travel expenses on time*
- *Keeping CRM updated in a timely manner*
- *Completing deal review artefacts and sharing them on time*

We make closure a habit by treating and closing everything in business and life as sales deals.

4. **I am following the sales process and best practices, yet the deal is not closing. What do I do?**
   The following three areas will help:
   ✓ Adopt the 3S Principle: Shraddha, Saburi, Sadhana. If results are not visible, focus on the fourth S, i.e., Surrender.

   Surrender to the universe in the form of a prayer: *'My team and I have done everything to close this deal. If this deal closure is for our highest good, please make it happen.* 🙏'

   Surrender to the universe in the form of acceptance: *'My team and I have done everything to close this deal. I am grateful to everyone for all the support. It's time to move on and explore other deals.* 🙏'

   ✓ Develop closure as a habit in all matters in life. This changes our vibrational frequency.
   ✓ Practice gratitude for what you have and visualization for what you want.

5. **How does meditation help in sales?**
   In my experience, meditation has decreased my *reactions* to situations. This

✓ helped me to be more centred, peaceful and empathetic.
✓ fueled equanimity in failures (rejection) and success
✓ increased my energy levels

6. How should I handle rejection in sales?

Implementing the following three attitudes will help in handling rejection:

✓ Higher purpose: Just as a soldier has a higher purpose of protecting the country, sales owners have a higher purpose of generating livelihood for their colleagues and economic growth for their country. When we remember this higher purpose, even big rejections will look small. 😇
✓ Meditation: Meditation decreases our reactions, thus enabling us to handle rejection well. I practise Vipassana meditation and it has done wonders for me in handling rejection and failures.
✓ Reframing.

The following question will help you reframe for a better future:

As a learning from this rejection, which three areas can I implement now to avoid this in the future?

7. The Use Case Selling four-part NICE model has many sub-principles. If I chose to implement only one among the many principles, which one would you recommend?

Closing a deal is like making the perfect mouth-watering dish. Let's say biryani. To make an ideal biryani in sales, one needs all the ingredients of Use Case Selling.

Even then, if you want to choose one principle, then choose metaphor because a metaphor:

✓ creates visual stories instantaneously
✓ makes the conversation memorable
✓ is easily relatable

Did you notice that I used a metaphor at the beginning of the answer? ☺

8. **Why has the Use Case Selling four-pillar NICE structure not been shared anywhere other than the book, e.g., videos, webinars and masterclasses?**
In the form of the NICE acronym, the four-pillar Use Case Selling structure can be understood easily. However, implementation requires diligence, discipline and profound work. Let's take an example.

Many of us watch sports such as cricket, soccer and tennis on television. Now imagine that we want to play the sport at the international level just by watching the game on television and without going through the entire training process. Is it possible? No.

In the same way, a short two-to-four-minute video on the NICE model or a one-hour session will trivialize the depth of Use Case Selling. Reading the book, completing all learning accelerators and filling the Use Case Selling checklist for a minimum of ten sales scenarios can help anyone better understand Use Case Selling. Covering Use Case Selling in a detailed training workshop is an alternative and can be leveraged once offered.

9. In B2B sales, business case/ROI is often required. How can Use Case Selling help?

A good business case requires articulation of needs, pain points and impact.
- ✓ Using the Mount Everest of Needs, first, identify and categorize the need across three categories: unmet, resistance to change and unknown needs.
- ✓ Among the identified needs, identify *high-priority* needs in consultation with the client. Each of these priority needs is a Unique Pain Point (UPP), which becomes a Unique Buying Point (UBP).
- ✓ Against each priority need,
  i. Map success stories in your current client base in the form of use cases and impact
  ii. Document qualitative impact and quantitative impact.

While the qualitative impact would be more straightforward, the quantitative impact requires both 'Yes Mindset' and 'Effort'.

Let me share an example.

During my MBA at IIM Ahmedabad, McKinsey came to coach us for our placement season. McKinsey's team suggested that we write a one-page CV with quantitative impact. We were taken aback because most of us, including me, had a five-to-ten-page CV. While it was challenging to reduce these pages to one page, it was more difficult to find impact in numbers. One student asked in a worried tone, 'As a project manager, I led teams and delivered projects. I don't have impact handy.'

The McKinsey team asked,

- What was the size of the team you led?
- What time was taken to complete the steps before you started the project?
- What time was taken to complete the steps after you finished the project?

The difference can be highlighted in hours, dollars or per cent improvement.

This example and a few other examples helped us believe we could show our work's impact quantitatively.

Like me, I hope this example reminds you that the quantitative impact can be created in a business set-up via 'Yes mindset' and 'Efforts'.

In many companies I have worked for, the presales, professional services and solutions teams have created a template for impact/ROI. We feed the client inputs to the template. The output is a clear demonstration of growth in key metrics over time.

The impact/ROI template decreases the sales cycle, shows your expertise and builds trust with the client.

Ask a question:

'Do you have a template to show the quantitative impact of your offering?'

10. **How does Use Case Selling map to Aristotle's Ethos, Logos, Pathos?**

Aristotle's three modes of persuasion	Use Case Selling's five mindsets	Use Case Selling's three tools
Ethos (Credibility)	Service mindset Thought Leader mindset	Rapport
Logos (Logic)	Unearthing new needs mindset	One thing
Pathos (Emotions)	Storytelling mindset Challenging the status quo mindset	Magical words: It's Like

List of Frameworks

A Handy List of Concepts, Frameworks and Accelerators in *The Ultimate Sales Accelerator*

The table below will act as an index to key concepts, frameworks and accelerators used in the book.

I hope this index guides you in revising concepts and thus accelerates your learning.

S. No.	Framework/ Accelerators	Chapter Number	Page No.
1.	The Magic Quadrant of GTM excellence	Prologue	xx
2.	Use Case Selling Four Pillars (NICE) Model	Chapter 2	12
3.	Mount Everest of Needs	Chapter 2	13
4.	Three Types of Insights	Chapter 2	20
5.	AI^2	Chapter 2	25

Notes

Prologue: Four Scenarios and Four Questions

1 'Nasscom sees flat growth in FY19 IT exports', Press Trust of India, Hyderabad, Deccan Herald, 20 February 2018, https://www.deccanherald.com/content/660583/nasscom-sees-flat-growth-fy19.html
2 'Indian Tech Start-up Ecosystem 2018: Approaching Escape Velocity', NASSCOM, https://nasscom.in/knowledge-center/publications/indian-tech-start-ecosystem-2018-approaching-escape-velocity
3 'Gartner Says 80% of B2B Sales Interactions between Suppliers and Buyers Will Occur in Digital Channels by 2025', https://www.gartner.com/en/newsroom/press-releases/2020-09-15-gartner-says-80--of-b2b-sales-interactions-between-su

Chapter 1: Why This Book

1 Life At Mindvalley, 'The 3 Most Important Questions to Ask Yourself', https://www.youtube.com/watch?v=f8eU5Pc-y0g

2 https://www.mindvalley.com/
3 https://www.the1thing.com/

Chapter 2: What is Use Case Selling?

1 Source: https://cogdogblog.com/2009/12/
2 Source: http://www.foxnews.com/entertainment/2018/
   05/01/can-hearme-now-verizon-guy-recalls-financial
   struggles-never-felt-secure.html
3 Mindvalley, 'How to Move People with Your Story |
   Lisa Nichols', https://www.youtube.com/watch?v= zLa
   N4bXFTMo
4 Source: https://en.wikipedia.org/wiki/Loss_aversion

Chapter 5: How Use Case Selling Works in B2C Scenarios

1 JoshuaG, 'Apple Music Event 2001-The First Ever iPod
   Introduction',   https://www.youtube.com/watch?v=
   kN0SVBCJqLs
2 'Case Study: Shot On iPhone 6 - Matthew McConnell
   and Sarah Markstaller', SlideShare, 5 March 2016,
   https://www.slideshare.net/MatthewMcConnell1/
   mktg340-case-study-shot-on-iphone-6-matthew-
   mcconnell-and-sarah-markstaller-59131990
3 Usman Qureshi, 'Apple's "Shot on iPhone 6" World
   Gallery Claims Top Prize in Cannes', iPhone in Canada,
   https://www.iphoneincanada.ca/news/apples-world-
   gallery-campaign-wins-at-cannes/

4 Arnab Dutta, 'How OnePlus Became the No.1 Smartphone in India', rediff.com, 8 August 2018, https://www.rediff.com/business/report/how-oneplus-became-the-no1-smartphone-in-india/20180808.htm
5 John Schroter, 'Steve Jobs introduces iPhone in 2007', https://www.youtube.com/watch?v=MnrJzXM7a6o

Chapter 6: How Use Case Selling Works in Personal Life

1 Captain of the Indian cricket team and recognized as the best batsman in the world (as on 6 April 2019).
2 For my readers who are unfamiliar with currency denominations used in India, 1 lakh = 100,000.
3 Men's Health India, 'Akshay Kumar Shares Fitness Secrets', https://www.youtube.com/watch?v= wNtU9 FyPKiU

Chapter 7: Why Is Use Case Selling So Effective?

1 Anrica, 'Neuroscience of Selling', Neuroscience of Selling, 12 October 2015, http://adaptiveneuroscience. com/2015/10/12/neuroscience-of-selling/
2 Source: https://darrenstehle.medium.com/your-actions-are-not-your-own-yourthree-brains-5c94a4ec016f
3 Source: https://media-assets-04.thedrum.com/cache/ images/thedrum-prod/s3-news-tmp-10557-lionel_ messi--2x1--940.jpg

4 Carmine Gallo, 'Ted Talks That Go Viral Have One Thing in Common', Forbes, 4 March 2016, https://www.forbes.com/sites/carminegallo/2016/03/04/ted-talks-that-go-viral-have-one-thing-in-common/#557219e517d6

5 Jim Camp, 'Decisions Are Largely Emotional, Not Logical', Big Think, 11 June 2012, https://bigthink.com/experts-corner/decisions-are-emotional-not-logical-the-neuroscience-behind-decision-making

6 'How Emotion Shapes Decision Making', https://intentionalcommunication.com/how-emotion-shapes-decision-making/#:~:text=The%20Brain%20Makes%20Decisions%20Based,which%20means%20to%20move%20%E2%80%93%20out.

Chapter 8: What Are the Five Mindsets That Can Fuel Excellence in Use Case Selling?

1 Julian Treasure, 'How to Speak So That People Want to Listen', TED, https://www.ted.com/talks/julian_treasure_how_to_speak_so_that_people_want_to_listen?language=en

2 Simon Sinek, 'How Great Leaders Inspire Action', TED, https://www.ted.com/talks/simon_sinek_how_great_leaders_inspire_action?language=en

3 Malcolm Gladwell, 'The Unheard Story of David and Goliath', TED, https://www.ted.com/talks/malcolm_gladwell_the_unheard_story_of_david_and_goliath

4 'Stories—Not Statistics—Are Memorable', 7 November 2015, https://speakingcpr.com/the-numbers-dont-lie-stories-not-statistics-make-you-memorable/

Chapter 10: How Does Use Case Selling Accelerate Virtual Selling?

1 Arnau Bages-Amat, Liz Harrison, Dennis Spillecke, and Jennifer Stanley, 'These Eight Charts Show How COVID-19 Has Changed B2B Sales Forever', McKinsey & Company, October 2020, https://www.mckinsey.com/~/media/mckinsey/business%20functions/marketing%20and%20sales/our%20insights/these%20eight%20charts%20show%20how%20covid%2019%20has%20changed%20b2b%20sales%20forever/these-eight-charts-show-how-covid-19-has-changed-b2b-sales-forever.pdf?shouldIndex=false

2 Many applications of the Rule of Three are given in the productivity section of my book *Small is Big*.

3 'How to Use the 7-38-55 Rule to Negotiate Effectively' MasterClass, 7 June 2021, https://www.masterclass.com/articles/how-to-use-the-7-38-55-rule-to-negotiate-effectively#quiz-0

4 Jon Michail, 'Strong Nonverbal Skills Matter Now More than Ever in This "New Normal"', Forbes, 24 August 2020, https://www.forbes.com/sites/forbescoachescouncil/2020/08/24/strong-nonverbal-skills-matter-now-more-than-ever-in-this-new-normal/?sh=1323019c5c61

5 Vanessa Van Edwards, '5 Secrets of a Successful TED Talk', Science of People, https://www.scienceofpeople.com/secrets-of-a-successful-ted-talk/

6 Temple Grandin, 'The World Needs All Kinds of Minds', TED, https://www.ted.com/talks/temple_grandin_the_world_needs_all_kinds_of_minds?language=en

7 Jane McGonigal, 'Gaming Can Make a Better World', TED, https://www.ted.com/talks/jane_mcgonigal_gaming_can_make_a_better_world

8 Simon Sinek, 'How Great Leaders Inspire Action', TED, https://www.ted.com/talks/simon_sinek_how_great_leaders_inspire_action?language=en

9 'Draw on Slides during a Presentation', https://support.microsoft.com/en-us/office/draw-on-slides-during-a-presentation-80a78a11-cb5d-4dfc-a1ad-a26e877da770

10 'Add Animation to Slides', https://support.microsoft.com/en-us/office/add-animation-to-slides%E2%80%8B-7db07067-4d78-40b5-bc87-5ff4f5ff6ff7

Thank You

I am very grateful to you for investing your valuable time to read this book. I trust that the learnings in this book will drive epic sales for you.

If this book has inspired you, please share it with others. Reviews help in informing and inspiring others, so I would request you to write a review on Amazon.

Thank you! 🙏

Acknowledgements

A book is a creative project that requires inspiration and participation from many avenues. I have been extremely blessed to have been able to write my first book in a comforting and inspiring ecosystem, where I was surrounded by guiding angels and wonderful experiences that have stood by me as I set out writing.

To begin with, I should talk about the book that completely changed my life. This book is *The One Thing* by Gary Keller and Jay Papasan. The beautiful question posited by this book transformed my thought processes. On 28 December 2017, I asked myself, 'What is the one habit I can develop in 2018, such that by developing it everything else would be easier or unnecessary?'

The universe gave me an immediate answer and I joined the 5 a.m. club. As I started waking up at 5 a.m., I found time to read many wonderful books. I began to spend thirty to forty-five minutes of my morning in the company of books and in 2018 alone, I read more than twenty books. I could clearly see how these books changed my life. They strengthened my resolve to become a published author and share my experiences. I am absolutely grateful to every author I've read because they inspired me to contribute to this vast world of books. Thank you Robin Sharma, Simon Sinek, Tim Ferris, Harv Eker, Sam Cawthorn and Vishen Lakhiani for your books, videos and words of inspiration that allowed me to explore newer perspectives . . .

My wife Ayesha (lovingly called Ashi) is a gift from God. She has been a loving and charming partner on the personal, professional and spiritual front, and a wonderful support system throughout the entire process. Interestingly, she was the first editor of the book. I would discuss every idea with her and she always had the patience, time and eagerness to hear me out and contribute. Ashi understood the fact that all of us are selling. She shared her thoughts and perspectives on the content, which were so fresh and enlightening because she doesn't come from a business sales background. Thank you Ashi for all the dedication and support you've given to this book and the journey.

Tahseen and Vishal are my ex-colleagues who took time off from their very busy schedules and provided inputs from the business-selling context. They found time to read every chapter and share their many observations over emails, WhatsApp and phone calls. Thank you Tahseen and Vishal for your valuable involvement in the project!

Vidushi, Vidisha and Joanna are three angels who patiently and diligently edited and refined the draft. It was great to see their commitment to the book and their drive to create a high-quality product. They were always available for review calls, be it hour-long discussions, calls at a short notice or calls that needed to be coordinated across time zones during my business travels! Thank you Vidushi, Vidisha and Joanna for your incredible support!

Thank you to everyone at Penguin Random House India for the excellent support provided in the course of the publishing of this book. Special thanks to Radhika, Ralph and Akangksha for their active, timely and valuable support. They were always available for discussions during the book design, editing and launch process.

I am thankful to my friends and associates who took the time to rate the ten book title options and helped me choose a suitable title for the book.

An author's vision is a reflection of his many experiences. In this regard, I am very grateful to my teachers, employers, clients, supervisors, colleagues, team members, friends and family who helped me live wonderful experiences that are now a part of the pages of this book.

My two sons, Tanish and Aarav, played a key role in my transformation into an author. In its simplest form, a book is a collection of stories and experiences. The time I spent with my sons, creating and telling stories, helped me a lot while writing the manuscript. Thank you Tanish. Thank you Aarav.

During the writing process, I got so many messages while reflecting, sleeping and meditating. Who was sending those messages? It was 'Up above' or 'the Universe'. To whatever question I asked, I got an answer. One key reason that this book addresses both business and life is because of the inspiration and guidance from 'Up above'. My heartfelt gratitude to 'the Universe' for guiding me 24/7.

Finally, I would like to express my heartfelt thanks and gratitude to all my readers. You have subconsciously inspired me to write this book. I love the saying that 'There is no friend more loyal than a book' and I hope that this book serves as a very loyal friend to you.

Thank you!